"*Immigration in the Court of Public Opinion* is that rare book that clears away the rhetorical fog obscuring the public's views on a hotly contested issue. With lucid data analysis and compelling logic, the book shows brilliantly that the polarization over immigration in the political elite is not matched in the opinions of the great mass of Americans, who cluster around a middle ground solidly anchored in core American values. The book is a paragon of the clarity of reasoning and evidence that good social science can bring to the public square."

Richard Alba, Graduate Center, CUNY

"*Immigration in the Court of Public Opinion* is a timely reassessment of Americans' attitudes about immigration policy, immigrants themselves, and their effects on many aspects of American society. Citrin, Levy, and Wright provide us with the most accessible, sophisticated, current, and analytically informed data available. This will immediately become the standard reference in the field, informing social scientists, policy-makers, media commentators, and private citizens, and illuminating countless public debates on one of the most important issues of our time. I have already used it in my own work on immigration policy."

Peter H. Schuck, Yale and NYU Law Schools

"Looking beyond the loud certainties of immigration policy debates, this book explores an alternate reality. With a deep analysis of extensive survey findings, Citrin, Levy, and Wright offer an authoritative account of public opinion on immigration across many dimensions. Most Americans, they find, express nuance, conflict, and uncertainty even as they embrace pluralism and generosity. An excellent distillation."

Roberto Suro, University of Southern California

Immigration in the Court
of Public Opinion

Immigration & Society series

Carl L. Bankston III, *Immigrant Networks and Social Capital*

Stephanie A. Bohon & Meghan Conley, *Immigration and Population*

Caroline B. Brettell, *Gender and Migration*

Jack Citrin, Morris Levy, & Matthew Wright, *Immigration in the Court of Public Opinion*

Thomas Faist, Margit Fauser, & Eveline Reisenauer, *Transnational Migration*

Adrian Favell, *The Integration Nation*

Eric Fong & Brent Berry, *Immigration and the City*

Roberto G. Gonzales, Nando Sigona, Martha C. Franco, & Anna Papoutsi, *Undocumented Migration*

Christian Joppke, *Citizenship and Immigration*

Grace Kao, Elizabeth Vaquera, & Kimberly Goyette, *Education and Immigration*

Nazli Kibria, Cara Bowman, & Megan O'Leary, *Race and Immigration*

Peter Kivisto, *Religion and Immigration*

Cecilia Menjívar, Leisy J. Abrego, & Leah C. Schmalzbauer, *Immigrant Families*

Ruth Milkman, *Immigrant Labor and the New Precariat*

Ronald L. Mize & Grace Peña Delgado, *Latino Immigrants in the United States*

Philip Q. Yang, *Asian Immigration to the United States*

Min Zhou & Carl L. Bankston III, *The Rise of the New Second Generation*

Immigration in the Court of Public Opinion

Jack Citrin, Morris Levy, and Matthew Wright

polity

Copyright © Jack Citrin, Morris Levy, and Matthew Wright 2023

The right of Jack Citrin, Morris Levy, and Matthew Wright to be identified as Author of this Work has been asserted in accordance with the UK Copyright, Designs and Patents Act 1988.

First published in 2023 by Polity Press

Polity Press
65 Bridge Street
Cambridge CB2 1UR, UK

Polity Press
111 River Street
Hoboken, NJ 07030, USA

All rights reserved. Except for the quotation of short passages for the purpose of criticism and review, no part of this publication may be reproduced, stored in a retrieval system or transmitted, in any form or by any means, electronic, mechanical, photocopying, recording or otherwise, without the prior permission of the publisher.

ISBN-13: 978-1-5095-5068-5
ISBN-13: 978-1-5095-5069-2(pb)

A catalogue record for this book is available from the British Library.

Library of Congress Control Number: 2022936093

Typeset in 11 on 13pt Sabon
by Fakenham Prepress Solutions, Fakenham, Norfolk NR21 8NL
Printed and bound in Great Britain by CPI Group (UK) Ltd, Croydon

The publisher has used its best endeavours to ensure that the URLs for external websites referred to in this book are correct and active at the time of going to press. However, the publisher has no responsibility for the websites and can make no guarantee that a site will remain live or that the content is or will remain appropriate.

Every effort has been made to trace all copyright holders, but if any have been overlooked the publisher will be pleased to include any necessary credits in any subsequent reprint or edition.

For further information on Polity, visit our website:
politybooks.com

To the next generation:

Sarah Citrin and Nina and Xander Thuesen
Isaac, Anna, Yvette, and Abraham Levy
Michael and Oliver Wright

Contents

Figures and Tables	viii
Acknowledgments	x
1 Who Are We Now?	1
2 Moderation, Malleability, and the Myth of Warring Camps	16
3 Motivations	41
4 Assimilation Then and Now	71
5 American Exceptionalism?	99
6 Conclusion	119
Notes	134
References	144
Index	151

Figures and Tables

Figures

1.1. The Changing American Demos 1980–2020	9
1.2. American Preferences for the Level of Legal Immigration 1965–2020	12
2.1. Number of Pro- and Anti-Immigrant Positions Taken	23
2.2. Immigration Support Score	26
2.3. Immigration Support Index among White Working Class	28
2.4. Immigration Support by Urban–Rural Divide	32
2.5. Immigration Support by Party	34
3.1. Economic Outlook and Desired Immigration Level	50
3.2. Group Prejudice and Desired Immigration Level	53
3.3. Egalitarianism and Desired Immigration Level	56
3.4. Immigrant Profiles	64
4.1. The Personal Importance of Ethnic and American Identities	82
4.2. Immigrant Generational Differences in Ethnic and American Identification	84
4.3. The Prioritization of Identities	86
4.4. What Makes Someone a "True" American?	91
5.1. Inflows and Border Control	104
5.2. Consequences of Immigration	107
5.3. Hostility to Cultural Pluralism	110
5.4. Predicting Government Support for Maintaining Minority Culture	113

Figures and Tables

Tables

2.1.	Summary of Immigration Items, ANES 2020	19
2.2.	Variation Across and Within Race/Ethnicity Groups	30
3.1.	Which Types of Immigrants Do People Prefer?	65
4.1.	How Important Is It to You That Immigrants...	96

Acknowledgments

This book illuminates what a nation of immigrants thinks about immigration. It shows that, along with suspicion and ambivalence, there is a solid core of acceptance. In documenting this with recent public opinion surveys, we benefited from the generosity of Emily Ekins, who shared the data from the Cato Institute's 2021 Immigration and Identity Survey. We owe a special debt of thanks to Gracielle Li for her skill and tenacity in helping to prepare this manuscript. We also are grateful to Matthias Leuprecht, Salihin Subhin, and Stephanie Peng for their research assistance. Eva Seto was indispensable in overseeing the administration of this project. Citrin thanks the Heller Fund of the Department of Political Science at Berkeley for its financial support for the project. Levy and Wright thank the Charles Koch Foundation for its generous support of this research.

1

Who Are We Now?

Every nation has a story, a collective answer to the "who are we, how did we get here, and what are we becoming" questions that are at the heart of its identity. Part of America's story is that it is a nation of immigrants, symbolized by the Statue of Liberty, arm outstretched in welcome. Yet every new wave of immigrants has provoked its share of anxiety and hostility as well. Immigration brings "strangers" into "our" land, and the human instinct is to view strangers with a mixture of curiosity, suspicion, and fear. The newcomers look different, speak differently, worship differently, and act differently. *They* will compete with *Us* for space, jobs, and, ultimately, for recognition and power.

How a nation of immigrants thinks and feels about immigration is the subject of this book. The core issues in immigration policy are how many should be allowed to come, who should be allowed to come, what should be expected of those who come, and what rights they should receive in return. Taken together, the US public's preferences about immigration speak to its conception of what it means to be an American.

We track public opinion over an era bookended by an extraordinary policy liberalization and the demographic transformation that ensued, and an effort by Donald Trump to close the door in a bid to "Make America Great Again." Openly ethnocentric, Trump singled out Muslim immigrants as potential terrorists and Mexicans as criminals, while rhapsodizing about welcoming idealized Norwegians. He cast immigration as a threat to American

1

Immigration in the Court of Public Opinion

jobs and values and called for a revised admissions policy based on a points system rewarding immigrants according to their skills (including speaking English) rather than their family ties.

As president, Trump issued a flurry of executive orders to ban immigration from Middle Eastern nations deemed a security threat, limit the number of H-1 visas for "essential workers," slow the access of foreign students to American universities, and end Deferred Action for Childhood Arrivals (DACA), the Obama-backed program allowing migrants under thirty who were brought to the United States illegally to remain and find work. Trump took special aim at illegal immigration, demanding a border wall, an end to "sanctuary cities," and harsher treatment and faster dismissal of asylum seekers. With Mexico's help, he capitalized on the pandemic to stem illegal entry.

During the Trump presidency partisan division on immigration hardened. As a result of movement among Democrats, attitudes shifted toward more support for increasing the level of immigration. Still, pushed into the background by Covid, immigration was not a salient issue in the 2020 election. Nevertheless, immediately upon taking office, President Biden sought to turn back the clock. Official rhetoric took on a decidedly pro-immigrant tone; for example, the terms "illegal alien" and even "assimilation" are now forbidden on official government documents.[1] Biden's own executive orders negated most of Trump's actions, including the ban on immigration from several Muslim-majority and select African nations, the construction of the border wall, the effort to curtail the DACA program, and the policy of sending asylum seekers back to Mexico before their hearing, among others.[2] Biden also has promised the major reforms that eluded his predecessors. But he too is finding the politically fraught situation at the Mexican border difficult to control and his predecessor's changes to asylum policy challenging to reverse.[3] The administration has equivocated, for example, about whether it will follow through on discontinuing a pandemic-era policy (Title 42) that permits removal of illegal immigrants without the opportunity to apply for asylum, a policy change that has publicly divided Democrats.

It is not our intention in this short book to follow these policy debates through the legislative, judicial, and regulatory labyrinths.

Who Are We Now?

Instead, we draw on a compendium of polls and academic surveys about immigration to see where the public stands on the more fundamental and enduring conflicts over immigration that shape the course of current conflicts. We track continuity and change in opinion, assess controversies about the structure and motivational underpinnings of immigration attitudes, compare the opinions of the country's main ethnic groups, and contrast Americans' views about immigration to those of citizens of other wealthy democracies.

We begin with a brief historical account of America's immigration regimes from the Founding to the present, emphasizing both the anxieties triggered by each wave of immigrants and the swing of the pendulum from inclusiveness to restriction based on ethnicity. Our review of public opinion then takes on the claim that a mean-spirited prejudice against immigrants, particularly Hispanics and Muslims, accompanied by resistance to cultural pluralism, dominates public opinion and policy in the United States. That is, we ask how much of the public shares Donald Trump's views on these issues.[4] We show instead that nativism, negativity, and polarization do not describe how the majority of Americans think about immigration. To be sure, there is a sliver whose views can be characterized as hostile, uniform, and intensely rigid. But by and large, the most accurate portrait of the public's views, we show, is one of ambivalence and complexity with a generally positive hue. Few line up on the same side of every issue, their policy attitudes are not especially consistent over time, and they make reasonable distinctions between categories of migrants.

Tribal or group-interested impulses do arise when people form opinions about immigration, but they often come into conflict with basic beliefs about law and order, assimilation, egalitarianism, and humanitarianism. Different aspects of immigration call forth different values, and thus the salience of these values and the context in which they are embedded will shape public attitudes, a factor that underpins the ambivalent and malleable nature of the responses of many.

Americans strongly favor assimilation over multiculturalism. But they also favor a thin form of assimilation that accommodates

Immigration in the Court of Public Opinion

space for minority cultures over the nativist's insistence on Anglo-Conformity. The evidence also shows that the new wave of immigrants from Asia and Latin America are assimilating; over time they increasingly identify as Americans, accept the value of English as the nation's common language, and express high levels of patriotism. The rapid spread of intermarriage is another important unifying mechanism. So, if America is being torn apart, immigrants aren't the culprit.

Is American opinion about immigration "exceptional"? We address this age-old question at a time when anti-immigrant sentiment also is churning the politics of European democracies, pushing official policies toward tightening borders and moving away from the embrace of multiculturalism in favor of the assimilation of newcomers. Using cross-national studies that include European countries and the "settler" countries of Canada, Australia, and New Zealand, we find clear evidence of American distinctiveness, sometimes unique and sometimes in concert with other settler nations, in its optimism about the consequences of immigration, openness to cultural pluralism (but *not* government intervention to sustain it), and, at least in the last decade, leniency toward illegal immigrants.

It is fair to ask why one should devote a whole book to public opinion about immigration when it is easy to point to large gaps between mass preferences and current policies. Despite widespread skepticism about the power of majorities in a political system with many barriers to change, when a problem becomes highly visible and salient, elites must pay attention to public opinion. To use the terminology of V.O. Key Jr., there may be a *permissive consensus* giving politicians the electoral leeway to act, or a *directive consensus* clearly warning against taking certain steps.[5] Key also points to the presence of *opinion dikes*, intense blocs of opinion that constrain change and, in the case of immigration, create difficulties for the Holy Grail of comprehensive reform.

No less important, the character of citizens' attitudes toward immigration speaks to the endurance and meaning of America's national identity and self-conception in the twenty-first century.

Will the ideal of a multi-ethnic nation united by a common attachment to universal values and love of country endure as diverse newcomers arrive, or will a competing image of America defined by the primacy of narrower identities come to dominate public thinking?

Contrary to the polarizing punditry, most Americans embrace neither nativism nor political multiculturalism. They are not hostile to foreigners or rising diversity, and they largely see immigration as a cultural and economic benefit to the nation. But they reject race-conscious policies that depart from the principle of colorblindness and equal treatment irrespective of race and ethnicity or that give a "free pass" to those who are in the country without permission. And they insist that immigrants adapt to their new environments enough to become self-sufficient.

The public's embrace of the American Creed – equality, individualism, and the rule of law – in the sphere of immigration policy is tempered by another traditional American value: pragmatism. The most hard-nosed opponents of increasing immigration tend to accept that some immigration is economically valuable and even culturally desirable, and that the only means of fully halting illegal immigration are inhumane or impractical. The most starry-eyed cosmopolitans usually recognize that fully open borders would court disaster in a world where security risks loom and large minorities of all people in the developing world say they would come to America if they could. Although partisan debates have polarized in the past twenty years, controversies about immigration in a nation of immigrants still largely play out between the proverbial forty-yard lines.

A Brief History of American Immigration Regimes

Immigration is the outcome of individual choices to move and the receiving country's collective decision to admit newcomers. Aside from a few philosophers and libertarians, there are no public proponents of "open borders"; every country has rules about who should be allowed to come, how many, and on

Immigration in the Court of Public Opinion

what terms. These decisions ultimately rest on beliefs about who "We" are, or, in the case of the US, what it means to be an American.

At the country's founding, Americans were a multi-ethnic mix, although the English were the most numerous and culturally dominant. As Gordon Wood writes, the founding generation realized that the attachments uniting Americans "could not be the traditional ethnic, religious, and tribal loyalties of the Old World" but would rest on a commitment to a democratic creed.[6] The Founders accepted that immigration was needed to facilitate territorial expansion and economic development but were confident that newcomers would absorb the Anglo-Protestant values at the core of the new nation's identity. With virtually no federal restriction on immigration and an easy path to citizenship, there was a steady but modest influx of immigrants from 1790 to 1830. But this inclusionary policy foundered when famine and economic distress resulted in a torrent of immigrants from Ireland and Germany arriving between 1830 and 1850. The Irish were suspected of loyalty to the Pope rather than their new country, the Germans of political radicalism, and both groups were deemed a threat to the dominant Anglo-Protestant values. *Nativism* – the rigid preference for descendants of the original Thirteen Colonies and an inflamed suspicion that other foreigners would destroy Americans' way of life – emerged and sparked the formation of anti-immigrant parties such as the Know Nothings and the adoption of measures to restrict immigration, slow naturalization, and pressure linguistic assimilation.[7]

After the Civil War, the confrontation over immigration turned to the Chinese who had begun to come to the Pacific West after the Gold Rush. Chinese labor was perceived as a threat to the livelihoods of white workers, stoking nativism cast in explicitly racist terms. In 1875, Congress passed the first substantive act limiting immigration, and in 1882 the Chinese Exclusion Act effectively ended Chinese immigration and encouraged the deportation of Chinese workers.[8] Resentment at job competition was clothed in blunt racial rhetoric of a sort that has long since disappeared even from the most ethnocentric corners of the American political

Who Are We Now?

scene, proclaiming the incapacity of the "yellow man" to live according to democratic principles.

Westward expansion and industrialization continued to attract labor to the United States, with millions from Eastern and Southern Europe heeding Emma Lazarus's invitation to the "huddled masses." This Third Wave peaked between 1900 and 1910 when nearly 10 million arrived. Once again it was the *character* as well as the magnitude of the influx that preoccupied nativists. The new inflows were dominated by people whose putative radicalism, lack of hygiene, and uncouth manners made them unsuitable for democratic citizenship.[9] At this juncture too, the rise of Social Darwinism and belief in eugenics buttressed the defense of a racial and cultural hierarchy based on the laws of natural selection. There was, many argued, a superior Anglo-Saxon culture, and lesser groups had to conform as the price of entry to America.

Still, until World War I, American presidents continued to adopt an open, though exacting, view of the requirements immigrants must meet. Theodore Roosevelt's views are emblematic of how mainstream leaders thought of absorbing newcomers. Roosevelt accepted that new blood could add to the nation's vitality but insisted that immigrants would have to shed many aspects of their original cultures and "learn to think, talk and be United States."[10] Roosevelt's insistence on assimilation nonetheless accepted that large-scale immigration benefited the US and left considerable latitude for immigrants to retain their private faiths and customs. The requirement was that immigrants adopt American values and retain no divided loyalties. The assumption was that most would.

But World War I intensified fear of Germany and accentuated concerns about national unity, shaking many Americans' faith in the melting pot and the feasibility of a laissez-faire approach to integration. Legislation in 1917, passed over Woodrow Wilson's veto, created, among other things, a literacy test requiring prospective immigrants to demonstrate basic reading comprehension in any language. Then, in 1921 and 1924, legislation provided for an annual limit of 150,000 who could immigrate and established national origins quotas based on the contribution of each nationality to the overall population of 1890.

7

Immigration in the Court of Public Opinion

Altogether, these changes favored immigrants from Northern and Western Europe over those from Southern and Eastern Europe. Immigration from Asia remained effectively nil.

Restrictive legislation essentially removed language and immigration issues from the national agenda for the next forty years. The immigrants who had already come could and did assimilate readily. Their status improved through economic mobility, political engagement, and a reduction of prejudice against them.[11] Earlier classifications of some Europeans as "Nordic and light" and others as "Mediterranean and dark" vanished.[12] Policy remained unchanged, but as World War II loomed and the need for national solidarity was manifest, nativist rhetoric faded and *cosmopolitan liberalism*, the older idea that American identity was not founded on ethnicity but open to anyone regardless of background who espoused the nation's creed, regained strength.

The Great Transformation

The fight against the Nazis and the Cold War struggle for the allegiance of newly independent nations in Asia made racism less tenable in policy and opinion. The passage of the Civil Rights Act of 1964 and the Voting Rights Act of 1965 completed the legal emancipation of African Americans. The Immigration and Nationality Act of 1965, one of the final acts of Lyndon Johnson's Great Society agenda, extended the principle of equality to dismantle the national origins quota system in American immigration. These twinned legislative revolutions have permanently transformed the contours of American politics and society.

The Act was the death knell for admission based on ancestry. National origins quotas were replaced by hemispheric caps using family reunification as the main basis for allocating visas, adding preferences for certain skills, and reserving a quota for refugees. The unintended consequences of the new rule were dramatic. Making family reunification the primary basis for visa preferences meant that the new immigrants would increasingly represent their immediate predecessors. A father from a particular country sent for his wife, children, and parents. Once they became citizens,

Who Are We Now?

spouses used the next level of preferences to send for their siblings. A process of "chain migration" then enabled each sibling to replicate the process of bringing in family members. This led to an unanticipated explosion of migrants, mainly from Latin America (especially Mexico), Asia, and Africa. Because these new immigrants and their offspring tended to be younger and more fertile than the native-born, the size of these ethnic groups grew exponentially.

According to an August 2020 report from the Pew Research Center,[13] the US foreign-born population reached a record 44.8 million in 2018, quadruple the number since 1965. In 1970, immigrants made up 4.8% of the US population; today they account for 13.7%, just slightly below the record share of 14.8% in 1890 when the much smaller number of 9.2 million immigrants lived here. The Census Bureau projects that, assuming no change in policy, the immigrant share of the population will reach 78.2 million by 2060, accounting for 18.8% of the total.[14] A nation of immigrants indeed.

Figure 1.1. The Changing American Demos 1980–2020

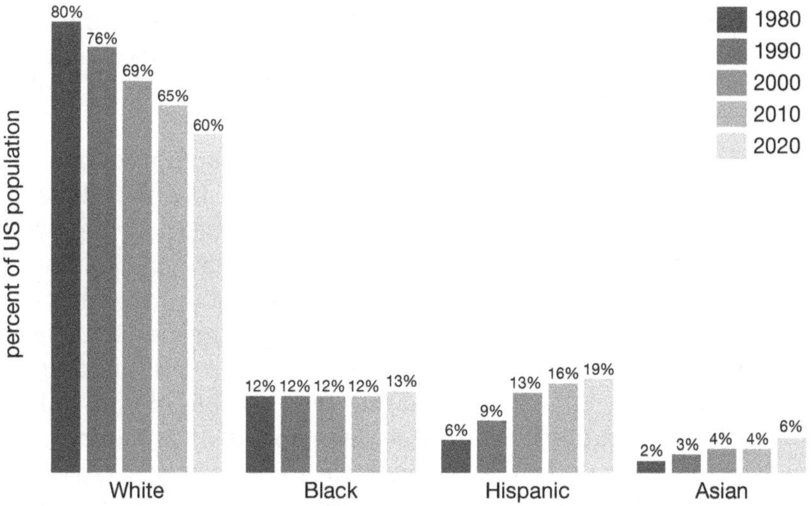

Source: Compiled with Census Bureau data

Immigration in the Court of Public Opinion

Immigrants from Europe and Canada now account for less than 10% of foreign-born residents, with Latin America and Asia accounting for more than 80%. Mexico (25%) is the top country of origin, followed by China (6%), India (6%), the Philippines (4%), and El Salvador (3%).[15] Since 2009, immigrants from Asia have outnumbered those from Latin America. In the wake of immigration reform, America is a changed society. As the Census data in Figure 1.1 show, the proportion of whites has steadily declined, and Hispanics and Asians have grown dramatically. However, the *fastest-growing* segment of the public is individuals with more than one race, the great majority of whom have a white parent and self-identify as both minority and white, undermining the widely circulated narrative that immigration has brought the US to the precipice of a "majority-minority" society.[16]

Alongside landmark changes in the terms of legal immigration, the number of immigrants coming without permission increased dramatically. In 2017, illegal immigrants were estimated to make up about one quarter of all foreign-born residents and more than 3% of the nation's population.[17] The problem is another unanticipated consequence of a well-meaning reform. Before 1965, migrants from Western Hemisphere countries such as Mexico and Canada were completely exempt from quota restrictions, and seasonal migrants from Mexico were allowed to work in the US as contract labor under the Bracero System, which was ended in 1964. The new hemispheric caps meant that official limits would be placed on the numbers who could come from Latin America. Due to the economic draw of jobs in America and the challenge of securing the long, porous southern border, illegal immigration has soared and increasingly preoccupied pundits and politicians, particularly (but not exclusively) within the Republican Party.

As we noted earlier, each wave of immigration has challenged Americans' notion of the "Circle of We."[18] America's founding on ideological principles (rather than in terms of blood and soil, as in some other nations), and its demographic diversity augmented by centuries of mass migration, have raised the stakes on the relationship between *ethnic* and *national* identity. This issue is largely settled among the immigrants from Europe and their

Who Are We Now?

descendants. Ethnic barriers have now melted away, and though people often refer to themselves as Irish, Italian, or Greek Americans there is little doubt that "America" enjoys the paramount loyalty. Whether this recurring hold of a transcendent common identity and concomitant allegiance to the ideals of liberty, equality, and patriotism will recur among the new wave of immigrants from Latin America and Asia is a question we take up in chapter 4. The nature of immigrant assimilation is a pressing question because of the emergence of multiculturalism as an ideology that legitimizes the primacy of ethnicity as the foundation of one's identity and advocates the preservation of immigrants' original cultures. The embrace of multiculturalist policy and ideology would amount to a departure no less radical than nativism from the traditional liberal assimilationist tenets of the American Creed, as ordinary Americans now understand it.

Public Opinion

What have ordinary citizens made of the changes wrought by immigration? Are they engaged and informed? Do they favor or oppose the changes or merely acquiesce? Are their opinions consistent in direction or complex and ambivalent? Chapter 2 explores these issues in detail. Here we make some brief preliminary observations that point to complexity or ambivalence in the public's thinking about immigration.

The longest-running survey question about legal immigration asks whether the number allowed to live permanently in the United States should be increased, decreased, or remain the same. Figure 1.2 shows the results of Gallup polls asking this question from 1965 on. When the Immigration and Nationality Law inaugurating the current inclusionary regime passed in 1965, immigration was at a low level. Still, 40% opted for the same, then-low level of immigration, 33% wanted a decrease, and only 9% chose more immigration. The apparent preference for less rather than more immigration has persisted until just recently, despite the entrenchment of government policies sustaining robust

Figure 1.2. American Preferences for the Level of Legal Immigration 1965–2020

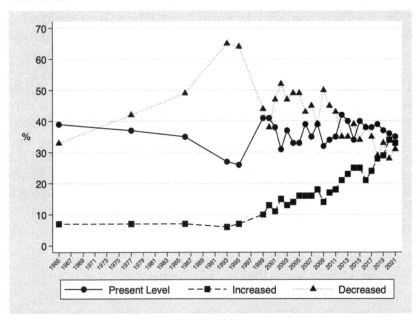

Source: The Gallup Index

immigration.[19] Indeed, anti-immigrant sentiment reached its peak during the recession of 1994, soon after an expansionist 1990 Act had taken effect.

In all surveys, a large bloc of respondents wanted "the same level" of immigration. Does this imply a casual response based on ignorance or indifference, or does it signify a greater acceptance of immigration as the level of admissions steadily grew? The answer matters for one's assessment of the level of anti-immigration sentiment and the existence of a gap between elite and mass opinion. As further evidence of ambivalence, the same polls often show support for decreasing immigration and overwhelming agreement that immigration is good for America. And many people find it difficult to choose between giving preference to family unification or to skills tailored to meet economic demands in the allocation of visas.

Who Are We Now?

The public does distinguish between legal and illegal immigration,[20] the latter being generally viewed unfavorably as a problem demanding government action. A January 2012 Gallup poll found for the first time since 2001 a majority (53%) saying that it was "extremely" important to "halt the flow of illegal immigrants into the United States," and two-thirds were dissatisfied with the government's handling of the problem. In 2001, 28% said they worried a great deal about the problem of illegal immigration; in 2021, the proportion had risen to 40%. Between 2004 and 2021, Gallup polls consistently showed that more than 75% of the public believed that large numbers of immigrants entering the United States illegally posed a critical or important threat to the country's vital interests. Even so, Americans are pragmatic about the complexities of how to treat the 12 million people living in the country without permission. There is pervasive recognition that mass deportation is not feasible without unacceptable breaches of humanitarian priorities and civil liberties. For over a decade, more than 60% have favored allowing illegal immigrants to remain in the United States and to have a pathway to citizenship provided they meet certain requirements. We return to these issues in the next chapter.

Public Opinion and Policy Reform

The fundamentals of policies governing admissions and illegal immigration have been in place, with just occasional tweaks, since the last major reforms passed in 1986 and 1990.[21] The national welfare reform of 1996 circumscribed immigrants' access to welfare benefits and other public services, while the Illegal Immigration Reform and Immigrant Responsibility Act of the same year ratcheted up enforcement.[22] In the decades since, pressure has mounted to reform a system viewed at all levels (including in public opinion) as "broken." Invariably, the impulse to reform has been preceded by optimism and followed by disappointment. So-called "comprehensive immigration reform" (CIR) proposals have tended to emphasize, to various degrees, the

Immigration in the Court of Public Opinion

following elements: 1) normalized status for the nation's illegal immigrant population (either a "pathway to citizenship" or "amnesty" depending on one's point of view); 2) increasing visas for high-skilled workers; 3) expanded provisions for temporary work programs designed to bring in much-needed low-skilled labor to the agricultural and seasonal sectors; and 4) stepped-up efforts to police the border and enforce prohibitions on hiring illegal immigrants.

Such proposals have been spearheaded by both Republican and Democratic presidents. CIR was a major goal of G.W. Bush's first administration, but it foundered on the shores of the 9/11 terrorist attacks. Renewed efforts toward the end of his second administration failed similarly. Barack Obama seized the initiative in 2009, but, to the reformers' chagrin, momentum faltered amid hostilities from both sides. Yet hope springs eternal, and even after the Democrats' "shellacking" in the 2010 midterms and the Republicans' seizing control of the House of Representatives, another effort was launched. President Obama announced a familiar-sounding suite of reforms, this time to include not only legislation but executive action if Congress should stall. Thus, although Republican Speaker John Boehner let the so-called "Gang of Eight" comprehensive immigration reform bill falter in the House after its strong 68–32 passage in the Senate, there were two significant policy changes. In the run-up to the 2012 election, the Obama administration initiated the broadly popular DACA program, offering temporary reprieve from deportation and renewable work permits for US-born children of illegal immigrants.[23] In November 2014, Obama went further, expanding DACA with an accompanying program – Deferred Action for Parents of Americans and Lawful Permanent Residents (DAPA) – to normalize the status of an estimated 4 million illegally present parents of children who are natural-born US citizens, along with an expansion of skilled immigration and increased spending on border security.[24] DACA has hit some legal headwinds and narrowly escaped a brush with bureaucratic death at the hands of the Trump administration, but it remains alive. Courts initially overruled the administration's attempt to shut it down, but

14

Who Are We Now?

currently (as of this writing) the program has been deemed "unlawful" by a Texas District Court. DAPA was dead on arrival in the courts and eventually rescinded by the Trump administration. There appears to be no talk of making another run at it.[25]

In all cases, optimism for these changes has been buoyed by substantial public support for most elements of the typical reform package. By the same token, many of the more extreme anti-immigrant policies pushed by the Trump administration – the so-called "travel ban" on entry from several mostly Muslim-majority countries, the aggressive separation of illegal immigrant families apprehended at the Southern US border, and Trump's signature "big beautiful" wall along that border – withered in the face of hostile majorities in the court of public opinion.

All of this suggests, at least on first blush, that any effort at reform, no matter how popular its provisions, is likely to fail. But this conclusion is premature: first, we must understand *what* exactly the public wants, and *why*. The chapters to follow are a systematic review of public opinion. We start from a few simple premises. In the absence of dramatic events or a campaign to focus public attention and concern, immigration is not a highly salient issue to most people. Nonetheless people do have preferences on the leading issues having to do with immigration policy. These opinions often are nuanced rather than tightly connected. They can be motivated by several competing considerations that come from the information people have about immigrants and immigration policy and by the multiple underlying values and identities they bring to these issues. The relative influence of Americans' manifold group identities and values can either lead to cross-pressures or sort people into antagonistic camps.

15

2

Moderation, Malleability, and the Myth of Warring Camps

Observers of immigration politics in America commonly portray two warring camps locked in a pitched battle over the nation's demography, economic structure, identity, and culture.[1] One side is portrayed as a hodgepodge of primarily white nativists, xenophobes, jingoists, cultural traditionalists, and atavistic nationalists who see immigration as a threat to the nation's way of life. Drawn from the ranks of the economically vulnerable and the culturally dispossessed, they harbor acute fears of social change, financial insecurity, and lost status – of being displaced or even "replaced" – in a more diverse country.[2]

On the other side is a coalition of left-leaning ethnic and racial minorities along with their well-heeled white cosmopolitan progressive patrons and businesses seeking cheap labor. Minorities supposedly support large-scale immigration because they are themselves immigrants, have close family and friends who are foreign-born, or feel a sense of solidarity and sympathy with both their own people and with non-whites generally. Upscale whites support it because they have bought into a system of values that subordinates the nation-state to cosmopolitan ideals and traditional liberal values to multiculturalist ideology. It just so happens that immigration also furnishes the professional class with the perks of a cheap, flexible immigrant labor force providing nannies, gardeners, and valet parking as well as the pleasures of ethnic cuisine – best enjoyed while basking in the satisfaction of being on the right side of history.

Moderation, Malleability, and the Myth of Warring Camps

Political parties, on this account, have positioned themselves to capitalize by mobilizing these competing forces into combat. Republicans have increasingly cast themselves as the mouthpiece of anti-immigrant populism and white working-class discontent. As the party's Reaganite coalition has weakened, free-market libertarians who support free trade and more open immigration have given ground to a more isolationist and protectionist wing that sees globalization as a threat to America's distinctive values and prosperity. In recent years, Democrats have become more muted in making broad appeals to the national interest and shifted, rhetorically at least, from New Deal-style class politics to a more race-conscious approach to privation and inequality. Two Democratic stalwarts who traditionally favored tighter restrictions on legal immigration and crackdowns on illegal immigration – labor unions and black civil rights groups – have shifted over time to an unambiguously pro-immigration position. For decades, the Democratic Party has been shedding its longstanding white working-class supporters – in effect trading white voters without a college degree for minority voters and especially highly educated whites – and this shift has been reflected in party polarization over immigration.

There is some truth in this interpretation. Class and race are quite predictive of people's attitudes about most immigration issues. The parties have become more distinct and polarized on immigration as their electoral bases have shifted. The metaphor of tribal warfare aptly describes a narrow but extremely influential pocket of elite activists and how they understand what is at stake. But if our goal is to understand mass opinion about immigration, the narrative of a polarized divide on immigration is deeply misleading. This chapter uses a combination of new analysis of recent survey data on immigration attitudes and a synthesis of existing research to demonstrate three inconvenient truths about the myth of all-encompassing warring blocs:

First, very few people hold uniformly "anti-immigrant" or "pro-immigrant" policy opinions. Most Americans instead endorse a mix of some policies that would increase immigration or expand immigrant rights and others that would reduce them. Almost none see immigration as a virtually unqualified good or

Immigration in the Court of Public Opinion

evil. Many Americans cherish the classic immigrant narrative of striving against all odds to create a new life, while also harboring anxieties about present immigration.[3] Here we demonstrate that Americans are not just of two, but many, minds about today's newcomers and how to greet them.

Second, when it comes to demographic groups that are often stereotyped as core constituencies within the pro- or anti-immigrant blocs, there is as much division of opinion *within* these groups as *between* them. Divisions over immigration are simply not reducible to race and ethnicity, class position, residential context, or even party identification.

Third, most Americans' opinions about immigration evolve over time and respond in sensible ways to different kinds of attempts to persuade them to adopt one position or another.

Americans' Opinions about Immigration are Moderate and Mixed

For evidence on the contemporary character of American public opinion about immigration, we rely primarily on the 2020 American National Election Study (ANES). This is both the most recent and the most comprehensive source of survey evidence available, and the ANES is generally considered as the gold standard of national surveys due to its sampling and its use of both in-person and online interviewing. Combining the pre- and post-election waves of the 2020 survey produced seventeen questions on immigration – eleven items on policy opinions, four soliciting beliefs about the consequences of immigration, and two "feeling thermometer" items that ask about people's warm or cold feelings (from the coldest possible score of "0" to the warmest possible score of "100") toward illegal immigrants and the Office of Immigration and Customs Enforcement. Table 2.1 summarizes the answers to these items.

These policies and perceptions cover a good deal of ground, albeit with some limitations worth mentioning. One is that they largely concern illegal immigration policy. The only exceptions

Moderation, Malleability, and the Myth of Warring Camps

Table 2.1. Summary of Immigration Items, ANES 2020

Policy Opinions

	Increase a lot	Increase a little	Keep same	Decrease a little	Decrease a lot		
Govt. spending on border security	*30*	*13*	34	**10**	**13**		
Level of immigration	**11**	**18**	43	*15*	*13*		

	Favor great deal	Favor moderate	Favor a little	Neither fav nor opp	Oppose a little	Oppose moderate	Oppose a lot
End birthright citizenship for kids of illegal immigrants	*15*	*9*	*2*	30	*3*	**12**	**29**
Building wall on border with Mexico	*25*	*9*	*3*	19	**2**	**9**	**34**
Allow refugees to come to US	**23**	**23**	**5**	34	*2*	*7*	*6*
Path to citizenship for illegal immigrants	**34**	**28**	**6**	18	*1*	*5*	*8*
Return unauthorized imm. to native country	*17*	*12*	*3*	31	**3**	**15**	**19**
Separate kids of detained immigrants	*3*	*2*	*1*	17	**2**	**13**	**62**

	Stay great deal	Stay moderate	Stay a little	Sent back a little	Sent back moderate	Sent back great deal
Children brought illegally sent back / stay	**47**	**30**	**11**	*2*	*5*	*5*

	Make all felons, deport	Guest worker program temporary	Allow to remain if meet conditions	Allow all to remain with no conditions		
Illegal immigration policy alternatives	*14*	15	55	**16**		

Consequences of Immigration

	Extremely likely	Very likely	Somewhat likely	Not at all likely			
Immigrants take away jobs	*9*	*17*	40	**35**			

	Decreases a lot	Decreases moderately	Decreases a little	No effect	Increases a little	Increases moderately	Increases a lot
Effect of illegal immigration on crime rate	*0*	*2*	*1*	43	**11**	**25**	**18**

	Agree strongly	Agree somewhat	Neither agree nor disagree	Disagree somewhat	Disagree strongly	
Immigrants good for economy	**23**	**37**	28	*9*	*3*	
Immigrants harm culture	*3*	*10*	24	**27**	**37**	
Increase crime	*4*	*22*	27	**21**	**26**	

Feelings about Immigration

	Coldest (0)	Cold (1-49)	Middle (50)	Warm (51–99)	Warmest (100)
Illegal immigrants feeling thermometer	*11*	*29*	25	**29**	**7**
ICE feeling thermometer	**14**	**26**	19	*33*	*8*

Notes: Displays percentage of all respondents who provided each response. Includes items from pre-election and post-election survey waves; all distributions weighted using full sample post-election weight. Feeling thermometers ask people to rate, on a scale from 0 to 100, how warm or cold their feelings are to the group in question (100 = warmest). Bolded entries are counted as "pro-immigrant" positions and italicized entries as "anti-immigrant." Minimum N = 7,065.

19

are the question about refugees, the "level of immigration" question, and the assessments of immigration consequences. Even the latter two aren't *explicitly* tied to legal immigration.[4] For all the talk about "merit-based immigration" during the Trump administration and earlier, there is no question pertaining to the appropriate balance between family reunification-based immigration and skills- or employment-based immigration. We will fill in these gaps in chapter 3, where we discuss opinions about legal immigration policy and delve into why people differentiate legal from illegal immigration, as well as the underpinnings of support for and opposition to "merit-based" reforms. For now, we note only that the heavy focus on illegal immigration policy stacks the deck *against* finding many Americans with mixed opinions that range from pro- to anti-immigrant.

A second limitation is that these questions exclude the most controversial progressive policy proposals on immigration aired during the 2020 Democratic primary season. Examples include abolishing Immigration and Customs Enforcement (ICE), decriminalizing illegal border crossings, supporting sanctuary cities, extending government benefits such as health insurance to illegal immigrants, and preserving (let alone expanding) the "diversity" visa lottery. All are deeply unpopular. For example, a Harvard-Harris poll from early 2017 found 80% of the public opposed to a standard conception of sanctuary cities.[5] Americans opposed the diversity lottery in a Reuters poll by 60–25. A PBS News Hour-Marist poll from December 2019 found 66% thought decriminalizing illegal border crossings a "bad idea," to 27% who thought it a good one, while in the same poll 62% thought "a national health insurance program available for immigrants who are in the US illegally" a bad idea, with only 33% deeming it a good one. Foreshadowing the sorts of complex patterns we will turn to in a moment, the PBS poll also found 2–1 support for a path to citizenship for illegal immigrants, whereupon, we would add, it would follow that these same immigrants would qualify for all federal assistance available to any other citizens.

For now, we simply wish to note that the apparent pro-immigrant skew of opinion in the ANES data, relative to the contemporary

Moderation, Malleability, and the Myth of Warring Camps

policy agenda, is partly a function of the poll questions that were asked. The breakdowns in Table 2.1 make it clear that most of the Trump-era Republican Party's stances on immigration were significantly out of step with public opinion. But they somewhat obscure how out of step many proposals favored by Democratic elites are as well. Although the results we present illustrate a great deal of sympathy among the American public for illegal immigrants and a desire to find pragmatic solutions, they should not for a moment lead us to believe that the public *favors* illegal immigration or sees it as unproblematic. In a 2021 Cato poll, for example, 71% of US adults said that illegal immigration is "unacceptable," even though a clear majority also favored a path to citizenship for illegal immigrants, and more supported addressing the problem by increasing legal immigration than by beefing up border security.

Considering in a holistic sense how people answer the variety of questions shows that there is a lot more nuance in people's attitudes than often is assumed, and that these patterns can be complex and counterintuitive. Only 29% of Americans want to increase the level of immigration (we note again the ambiguity of the middle "keep it the same" response; see chapter 1), but 51% support taking in refugees, and even larger majorities take the pro-immigrant side on policy debates that pertain to how to treat illegal immigrants in the country – this despite the fact that only 36% of Americans express even mildly "warm" feelings toward illegal immigrants. Sometimes things verge on contradiction: a clear plurality of the public favors increased spending on border security, and few want to reduce it, but a plurality also opposes building a wall on the border with Mexico. Likewise, there is overwhelming support for creating a pathway to citizenship for illegal immigrants, but one finds far less opposition to returning illegal immigrants to their native countries – a polite way of saying deportation. At the same time, many of those who *do* favor deportation in the abstract would clearly prefer less draconian alternatives when those alternatives are presented, with only 14% wanting to further criminalize illegal immigrants by declaring them felons and summarily deporting them.

Immigration in the Court of Public Opinion

Predictably, children elicit a great deal of sympathy. Only a sliver of the population wants to deport children brought illegally to the US. This sentiment conforms to the supermajority support for the Obama administration's Deferred Action for Childhood Arrivals (DACA) program, which the Trump administration sought unsuccessfully to reverse and which remains in legal limbo. Indeed, the Trump administration's move to separate apprehended children from parents was so unpopular that it was rescinded, and administration officials sought to deflect blame by insisting that President Obama had in fact initiated this policy. Yet it is also true that opposition to ending birthright citizenship for US-born children of illegal immigrants fails to garner a majority. So, while most of the public dislikes policies that seem at odds with humanitarian treatment of child migrants, many of them clearly draw the line at citizenship, despite the long-running understanding that the 14th Amendment guarantees that anyone born on US soil is automatically an American citizen.

Some of these questions probe people's evaluations of groups, institutions, and even immigration itself rather than their evaluations of policies. On this front, 60% of Americans do not have "cold" feelings about ICE, but 60% also do not have cold feelings about illegal immigrants. Questions about the impact of immigration on the economy, the culture, and crime register far more positivity than negativity. Yet most respondents believe that illegal immigration will increase crime rates "at least a little," and only 35% say it is "not at all likely" that immigrants will take jobs from natives, although 40% give the non-committal "somewhat likely" response.

What all this indicates is that many Americans hold a mix of pro- and anti-immigrant attitudes. To examine this directly, we added up for each respondent the number of pro-immigrant positions taken across the gamut and separately the number of anti-immigrant ones. Distinguishing the pro- and anti- questions is necessary because many respondents took a good number of positions that struck us as falling in between – neither obviously pro-expansion nor pro-restriction. For example, what about the large number of people who wish to keep the already quite

22

Moderation, Malleability, and the Myth of Warring Camps

high level of immigration about the same? And is saying that immigrants are "somewhat likely" to take jobs a pro- or anti-immigrant response? Our coding decisions are displayed in Table 2.1, where bolded figures indicate pro-immigrant and italicized anti-immigrant responses. We left ambiguous responses such as "keep it the same" on the level of immigration question out of both indexes. In practice, one can quibble with our choices and slice things in any number of plausible ways without meaningfully changing the conclusions that follow.

Figure 2.1 displays these counts as a histogram – a visual representation of what proportion of respondents receives each score on the index – for pro- and anti-immigrant positions. It brings into relief the limited degree of polarization. Fewer than 6% took consistently pro-immigrant positions, but, just as notable, fewer than 2% failed to take a single pro-immigrant position. Eighty-six percent took at least four pro-immigrant positions, in

Figure 2.1. Number of Pro- and Anti-Immigrant Positions Taken

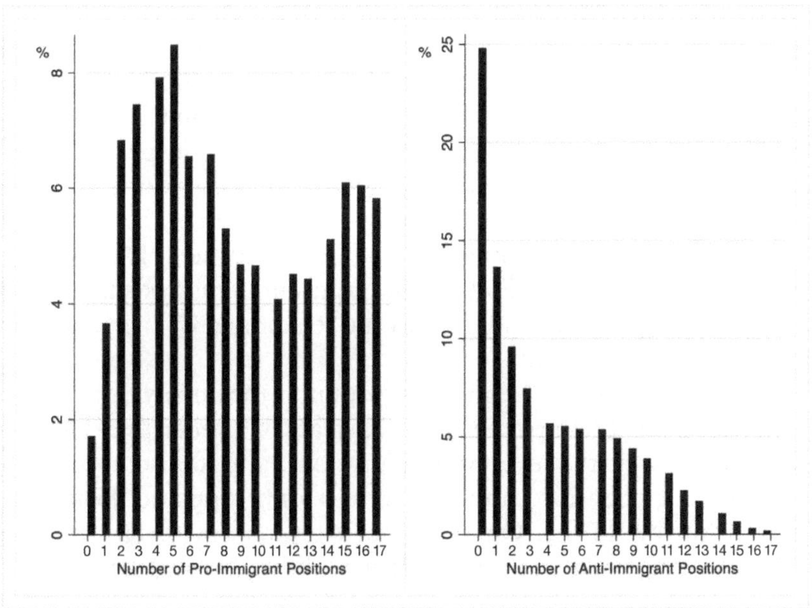

Source: ANES 2020

Immigration in the Court of Public Opinion

effect directly bucking the Trump administration on these items. But only 18% took fifteen or more pro-immigrant positions.

Although only a small fraction of the public was consistently on the pro-immigrant side of these items, a more sizable minority didn't take a single anti-immigrant position, and over a third took no more than one. The other side's die-hards are not any more numerous: there is only a tiny constituency backing consistent anti-immigrant positions. The number taking all seventeen anti-immigrant positions is essentially a rounding error, 0.25%. Perhaps even more striking, 95% of the sample takes fewer than twelve anti-immigrant positions, leaving only a small minority that is regularly in line with the views propounded by former President Trump.

The point here is not that Americans are broadly pro-immigrant in the sense that self-styled progressives have defined it. Doubtless their support for immigration is far greater than one might expect given the frequency with which terms such as nativist, racist, and xenophobic are thrown around in the current discourse. But as we noted earlier, there is majority opposition to policies such as sanctuary cities, decriminalization of illegal border crossing, and other progressive policies such as the provision of welfare benefits even to legal immigrants.[6] Rather, the point is that most of the public lands somewhere in the middle of the spectrum and on different sides of the spectrum on different questions, holding some pro-immigrant attitudes, some anti-immigrant attitudes, and no small number of attitudes that fall in between. The average person in the 2020 ANES took 4.5 anti-immigrant positions and 8.8 pro-immigrant positions, with the remaining 3.7 being neither pro- nor anti-immigrant.

Some examples of the mixes of opinion that many Americans hold can make these patterns less abstract. Consider that 50% of those who want the level of immigration reduced also supported a path to citizenship, and this group only opposed birthright citizenship by 45–24. On the other side, one in seven of those who wanted *increased* immigration did not support a path to citizenship, and almost one in three supported deporting illegal immigrants. Supporters of a pathway to citizenship also

Moderation, Malleability, and the Myth of Warring Camps

leaned toward spending *more* on border enforcement by 44–23. Thirty-two percent of them expressed cold feelings toward illegal immigrants (<50) and another 23% neutral feelings; 49% of them expressed warm feelings toward ICE and only 34% cold feelings.

Bear in mind, too, that even those very few who answered the ANES immigration questions in a uniformly or nearly uniformly pro- or anti-immigrant direction were not necessarily expressing *strong* support for these alternatives. To say one wants to reduce immigration "a little" is not really hewing to the Trump administration's repeatedly articulated position on the matter, which was that it should be reduced by a lot – by half in some of the proposals Trump supported, or altogether for a time in some of his campaign literature. Nor is saying you wish to increase immigration "a little," or that you "somewhat" support a path to citizenship for illegal immigrants, truly indicative of alignment with the Democratic Party platform, which enthusiastically endorses both. In other words, the approach taken in Figure 2.1 understates the degree of moderation in public opinion about immigration. A different approach, which accounts for the extremity and intensity of opinion, is to create a scale of immigration support that averages responses to all seventeen questions for each respondent, with each question coded to range from zero to one, where one indicates that the respondent provided the most pro-immigrant response available (e.g. strongly support birthright citizenship, strongly agree that immigration is good for the economy) and zero indicates the most anti-immigrant response possible (e.g. reduce immigration levels a lot, strongly agree that immigration causes crime). The distribution of the immigration support measure for the full sample is shown in Figure 2.2.

Remarkably, the extreme anti-immigrant position is regularly taken by only a tiny fraction of the public. Only 3.5% of the sample scores 0.2 or lower. Once again, pro-immigrant positions are far more prevalent. But only 0.5% of the public took the most pro-immigrant position on all items, less than 7% scored above 0.9, and 21% scored above 0.8. This means that 75% of Americans scored between the two lowest fifths of the scale, or might we say between the twenty-yard lines. A more balanced set of questions that asked about

25

Figure 2.2. Immigration Support Score

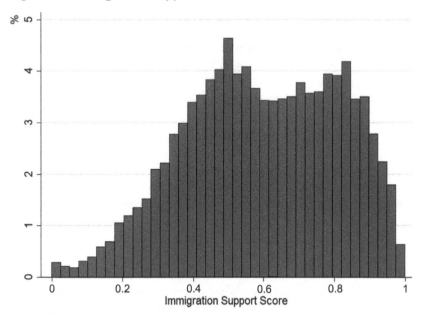

Source: ANES 2020

relatively unpopular policy initiatives from the progressive wish list would no doubt have rounded out the curve's symmetry and left even fewer closer to the extremes. But even with the limitations of the available data, it should be quite clear that very few Americans conform to the pro- or anti-immigrant stereotypes that abound in standard accounts of contemporary mass politics. The great majority hold mixed opinions and tend toward moderation. Almost all stray far from the poles represented by activists and, increasingly, the positions taken by party leaders. Only a tiny minority could sensibly be described as "nativists" in the sense described in chapter 1.

Heterogeneity and Moderation in Key Groups

Perhaps we would find more evidence of clearly pro- or anti-immigrant positions if we focused on the specific constituencies

Moderation, Malleability, and the Myth of Warring Camps

often highlighted by pundits. Here we examine this possibility by focusing on the education (a common proxy for class), age, race, geographic, and partisan cleavages that animate these narratives.

Education

No group has received more attention in this regard than the white working class. Supposedly marked by racial resentment to begin with and riled by fears of displacement in a globalized economy, they have been singled out as a force ready to be mobilized by anti-immigrant entrepreneurs. For simplicity's sake, we divide our sample by whether they have earned a college degree. Unsurprisingly, whites without this credential are indeed significantly more opposed to immigration than whites with a college degree. Working-class white voters score on average roughly one-eighth (0.12) of the full immigration support scale lower than the college educated. They take three fewer pro-immigrant positions, and two more anti-immigrant positions than their better educated white counterparts.

But these differences across class groups are dwarfed by the diversity of opinion *among* the white working class. The interquartile range – the distance, in scale terms, between the respondents scoring in the 75th percentile and the respondents scoring in the 25th – on the immigration support scale is 0.31 (0.37–0.68). The interquartile range is a useful metric because it tells us something about the breadth of consensus. Three-fourths of Americans are less anti-immigrant than the bottom of the interquartile range (25th percentile), and three-fourths are less pro-immigrant than the top of the range (75th percentile) on the immigration support index. So, in the present case, only 25% of whites without a college degree fell below 0.37 on the scale, while 25% scored above 0.68, and half the sample fell in between. The 25th percentile white working-class respondent took seven fewer pro-immigrant positions than the 75th percentile (3 to 10) and eight more anti-immigrant positions (9 to 1). It is clearly a mistake to speak of the white working class as though it were anything close to a unified bloc on immigration. Rather, its

Immigration in the Court of Public Opinion

internal diversity is much greater than standard narratives have appreciated. Moreover, looking at Figure 2.3, modest average differences between class groups obscure the fact that most white working-class voters hold complex mixes of pro- and anti-immigrant opinions, along with some neutral ones.

The mean and median of the distribution are right smack in the middle: 0.5 and 0.52 respectively. Fully 95% of the sample score above a 0.2, signaling that these voters are hardly in lockstep with the Trump agenda. Less surprising, given the standard narrative, is that only 12% score above 0.8. But this means that over 80% of white working-class voters fall in the middle of the distribution. Only 2% of this group take the pro-immigrant side on none of the items, while 3% take uniformly pro-immigrant positions. More than half – 52% – take at least six pro-immigrant positions (i.e., the pro position on more than a third of the items); 30% take the pro-immigrant position on more than half. On average, white

Figure 2.3. Immigration Support Index among White Working Class

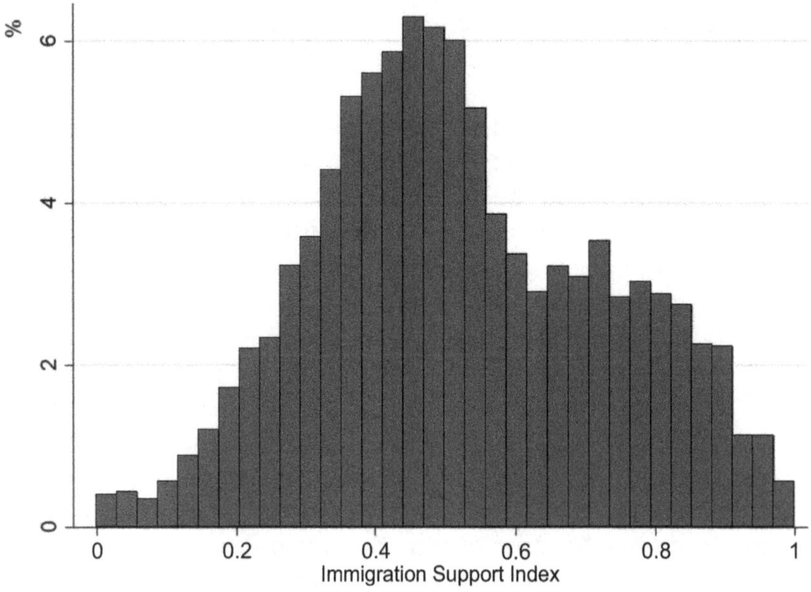

Source: ANES 2020

Moderation, Malleability, and the Myth of Warring Camps

working-class respondents took the *pro*-immigrant side on 6.9 out of the seventeen items. The standard conception of unalloyed white working-class opposition to immigration is further undermined when we look at the number of anti-immigrant positions taken. The average respondent in this group took only 5.3 out of the seventeen; that is, she took the anti-immigrant position on less than a third of the items. Eighty-six percent of white working-class respondents took fewer than ten anti-immigrant positions. A mere 3% took as many as twelve. None of this is in keeping with the portrayal of this group as a hotbed of xenophobia and nativism.

Age

Immigration politics, like many other matters that touch on race and ethnicity, is frequently discussed in terms of a generational divide between older, more conservative, cohorts and younger Americans who are less nationalistic and more in tune with "diversity, equity, and inclusion." To examine this, we divide the sample into three groups: those 18–40 (millennials and younger), 41–65 (Gen X), and 66+ (Boomer and Silent Generations). Although the youngest cohort leaned slightly more pro-immigrant than the two older ones, the average differences turned out to be quite muted, and we found no difference whatsoever between the two older cohorts. The youngest group took an average of 9.6 pro- and 3.5 anti-immigrant positions, compared to an identical 8.4 and 5.0 apiece among each of the two older groups. The two older groups average only approximately 0.07, or one-third of a standard deviation, lower than the youngest on the immigration support index. Visually, the distributions of opinion within each group are almost indistinguishable, so we spare the reader these graphics. Youth is predictive of somewhat less opposition to immigration. But the differences are small.

Race

Non-white groups are often assumed to be decidedly pro-immigrant. This is especially true of Latinos and Asians, putatively because

Immigration in the Court of Public Opinion

larger numbers of these groups are themselves foreign-born or children of immigrants. This narrative persists even though Hispanic voters were, if anything, more supportive of Trump in 2016 than of Romney in 2012 and far more supportive of Trump in 2020 than of any GOP candidate since George W. Bush in 2004. As Table 2.2 shows, there are indeed meaningful, if again relatively modest, average differences between racial groups in the immigration support index and the number of pro- and anti-immigrant positions. The biggest differences are between Hispanics and whites. Hispanics take an average of 2.3 more pro-immigrant positions and 2.5 fewer anti-immigrant positions than whites, and they score 0.13 higher on immigration support.

But, once again, differences among Hispanics dominate the differences between them and other groups. The interquartile ranges suggest that there is almost as much heterogeneity among Hispanics as among whites on two of the three indicators, the notable exception being anti-immigrant positions, which the great majority of Hispanics appear to be reluctant to take. Here the focus on illegal immigration and Trump-era policies probably enhances differences between groups. Still, there is far more difference between the 25th and 75th percentile within each minority group than between that group's average and that of whites.

Table 2.2. Variation Across and Within Race/Ethnicity Groups

Racial Group	Immigration Support Index		Pro-Immigrant Positions		Anti-Immigrant Positions	
	Mean	I-Q Range	Mean	I-Q Range	Mean	I-Q Range
White	0.56	0.41–0.77	8.4	4–13	5.1	1–8
Black	0.61	0.53–0.76	8.9	5–12	3.7	1–5
Hispanic	0.69	0.56–0.82	10.7	5–14	2.6	0–4
Asian	0.63	0.49–0.77	9.9	5–13	3.6	0–6
Native American	0.57	0.45–0.71	8.1	4–11	4.9	1–6
Multiracial	0.64	0.49–0.80	9.8	4–13	3.5	0–6

Geography

Accounts of the immigration divide also draw heavily on geography or place of residence. Typically, the cosmopolitans of the cities and inner upscale suburbs are pitted against small-town America and its exurbs and outlying rural areas. A large body of research has examined the effects of geographic proximity to immigrants and found little evidence of the contrary hypothesis that familiarity in largely urban gateway settings breeds contempt.[7] These narratives about the impact of geography are closely entwined with categories we have already considered – race and class. But space and context may have effects on the way people think about immigration that go beyond differences in the demographic composition of the population. To investigate, we use a variable in the ANES that codes whether individuals reside in rural areas or small towns ("non-urban," 40% of the sample) versus suburbs or cities ("urban," 60%).

Here, we find small but meaningful average differences across these geographically defined groups. Urbanites score 0.09 higher on the immigration support index than non-urbanites, take an average of 2.1 more pro-immigrant positions (9.7 vs. 7.6) and 1.7 fewer anti-immigrant positions (3.8 vs. 5.5). Yet once again, the internal heterogeneity of these groups, and the mixes of opinions that most individuals hold, belie any reductionist notion that spatial context strongly determines opinions about immigration. Figure 2.4 tells the story. Whereas the distribution of immigration support skews higher for urbanites than non-urbanites, both groups show a great degree of heterogeneity, and non-urbanites in fact also have a *pro*-immigrant skew – just a less pronounced one than among urbanites.

The interquartile range for the number of pro-immigrant positions held by non-urbanites is again wide, 4–12, and among urbanites equally wide but shifted two units, 6–14. The respective ranges on anti-immigrant positions are 1–9 and 0–7. In contemporary American politics the rural–urban divide surely matters. And this carries over to immigration politics. But the evidence once again shows that there is much more diversity of

Figure 2.4. Immigration Support by Urban–Rural Divide

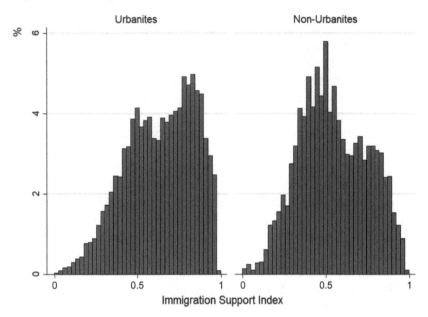

opinion within these groups than difference of opinion between them.

Partisanship

The most important divide in American politics is partisanship, as the daily references to polarization bordering on tribalism show. Democrats have long been viewed as the party of immigrants, though the party's southern wing and affiliation with the labor movement muddied the picture for much of the last century. Until recently, the Democratic and Republican parties were hardly Tweedledee and Tweedledum on immigration, but they did agree on many priorities. Both saw legal immigration as vital to the nation's prosperity. Both agreed that tough measures were needed to stem the flow of illegal immigrants, even though both also came together in the last "comprehensive immigration reform" in 1986 – the Immigration Reform and Control Act, which gave legal

Moderation, Malleability, and the Myth of Warring Camps

status to an estimated 2.7 million illegal immigrants in exchange for an employer sanctions regime that was seldom seriously enforced.

As recently as 2013, there was bipartisan support for a comprehensive immigration reform bill that would have paired a large-scale amnesty with stepped-up enforcement measures and changes to the legal immigration system that would exchange some family-based visas for skills-based admissions. But in the past decade, the two major parties have again moved far apart on immigration, a process that was already evident during the Obama administration but took off dramatically with the nomination of Donald Trump.[8] Few Republican leaders now openly support mass legalization programs, though many continue to back more targeted ones such as DACA. Few Democrats are willing to publicly countenance strong measures to contain illegal immigration, even if they reject the accusation that they are for "open borders," and few would hazard support for cutting family-based visas even if the cuts are offset by skills-based immigration. And while most Republicans – including Trump, at times – continue to praise legal immigration, the GOP's rhetoric has turned harsh, while Democrats seem to find it ever more difficult to say illegal immigration is a problem, or even call it by any name that indicates any law has been broken. The nomenclature wars sometimes veer into Orwellian territory. Interviewed on CNN's State of the Union morning program while he was mayor of Chicago, Rahm Emanuel described illegal immigrants as "those who may not have all their papers in order."[9]

These changes are often seen as reactions to bottom-up pressures from key constituencies in each party's coalition – the white working class, which is increasingly Republican, and minority groups and immigrants themselves, who have tended to vote Democrat. Given the great heterogeneity of opinion within these groups, partisan repositioning on immigration is unlikely to be driven primarily by these changes, or, at least, they must be only a part of the story. Regardless, given that the parties have staked out such different positions on immigration, standard theories of elite influence on public opinion would suggest that we should find Democrats and Republicans in the electorate

33

quite far apart on these issues. In fact, we do find considerable partisan polarization. But the common caricature of each party's faithful ignores substantial variation among both Democrats and Republicans.

As Figure 2.5 shows, Democrats are not in lockstep on the "pro-immigrant" side of contemporary partisan debates, and Republicans are surprisingly out of step with the Trump agenda. Democrats' average immigration support score (.73) is of course a great deal higher than Republicans' (.45). And Democrats take the pro-immigrant side on twice as many policies (11.9) than Republicans do (5.8), while Republicans take more than three times as many anti-immigrant positions (7.3) as Democrats (2.0). But a third of Democrats take ten or fewer pro-immigrant positions – meaning they do not directly buck the Trump line on at least seven. Only 12% of Democrats take the pro-immigrant position across the board. The dispersion of opinion is even greater when it comes to Republicans. More than a third take at

Figure 2.5. Immigration Support by Party

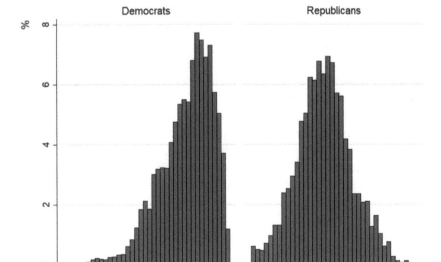

Moderation, Malleability, and the Myth of Warring Camps

least seven *pro*-immigrant positions, 85% take at least three, and only 2% take none. A mere 0.6% take the anti-immigrant position across the board, and 87% of Republicans take no more than ten such opinions. Fully 62% of Republicans take the anti-immigrant position on fewer than half the issues.

Do things differ if one considers the intensity of partisan identification? Not much among Democrats. The slightly more than half of Democrats who say they identify "strongly" with the party differ hardly at all from those with weaker stated attachments. Among Republicans, strong identifiers (again approximately half of all who identify as Republicans) are notably more in favor of restricting immigration than others, taking on average two fewer pro-immigrant positions (4.8 vs. 6.7 among other Republicans) and 2.5 more anti-immigrant positions (8.6 vs. 6.1). While Trump's agenda on immigration seems to have been unpopular among all Democrats across the board, there is some evidence that strong Republicans were likelier to follow the leader on these issues than were the half of Republicans with weaker partisan attachments. Nonetheless, after four years of the Trump presidency, even strong Republicans directly bucked his immigration agenda on no small number of immigration issues.

Differences between the parties notwithstanding, opinions within each party are quite diverse. Some examples help make this concrete. In the 2020 ANES, only 44% of Republicans support reducing immigration even "a little," while barely over a fifth (21%) support reducing it a lot. Only 46% of Democrats support increasing immigration levels, and only 19% by "a lot." In both parties, "keep it the same" is the plurality response by a wide margin. Only 58% of Democrats oppose trying to deport illegal immigrants, and only 55% of Republicans support this. Only about a third of each party takes the "strongly" position in this regard. Republicans also favor a path to citizenship by 57–24, while Democratic support is overwhelming for the idea of a path to citizenship, with 80% in favor. However, only 27% of Democrats support a path to citizenship without conditions – a blanket amnesty. A *majority* within both parties (59% of Democrats and 52% of Republicans) prefer a path to citizenship

Immigration in the Court of Public Opinion

for immigrants who meet the sorts of conditions outlined in recent efforts at comprehensive immigration reform over a blanket amnesty, temporary work permits, or mass deportation – which is favored by less than a quarter of Republicans.

The Malleability of Opinion

In addition to holding largely moderate and mixed opinions on immigration, Americans can and often do change their minds. This is still disputed by some because of studies that claim to find little responsiveness of immigration attitudes to information. The usual explanation is that immigration attitudes are so deeply rooted in core social identities and group attachments that they are resistant to change, essentially fixed.[10] But the fact that some studies fail to find shifts in attitudes toward immigration is hardly evidence for fixity. Others do find considerable evidence of change, and the shifts in aggregate opinion that we alluded to in chapter 1 (more below) firmly refute the contention that people's opinions don't change in response to the world around them. The public is not nearly as dug-in on immigration as some accounts suggest.

Some of the strongest evidence on whether people change their minds about immigration comes from panel data – surveys that interview the same people at least twice. Prior research[11] looks at just such data – the level of immigration item in a General Social Survey (GSS) three-wave panel from 2006–08–10. It turns out that a person's opinion about the level of immigration in any of the three waves was only modestly predictive of opinions in the other waves. The correlation between opinions in any two waves was approximately 0.5. More concretely, grouping respondents by whether they favored an increase of any kind, a decrease of any kind, or keeping things the same, about a third of respondents changed opinions in any two-year window. Fewer than half remained in the same broad category in all three waves. A mere 9% said they wanted to reduce immigration "a lot" all three times, and only about 1% wanted to increase it all three times. This suggests that there is at most a very small constituency on

Moderation, Malleability, and the Myth of Warring Camps

either side that is unalterably committed to changing the volume of immigration.

How do immigration attitudes compare to other types of opinions? The level of stability here was no higher than in many other issue domains that do not tap into deep-seated group identities – various types of government spending, for example. In other words, opinions about the level of immigration moved around about as much as opinions about whether to spend more, less, or about the same on education, social security, and other government priorities. Moreover, opinions about immigration moved around a lot more than did views on other culture war-type issues, such as marijuana legalization and gay marriage, and on most racial issues, such as government efforts to improve the condition of blacks.

To update these findings, we looked at the most recent high-quality panel data on the level of immigration item, again from the GSS. In 2020, the GSS re-interviewed a few hundred respondents who had been part of the 2016 and 2018 samples (however, no respondents were interviewed in both '16 and '18). Well into the Trump era, the stability coefficients of immigration attitudes have remained about the same as they were more than a decade ago and only slightly higher than they were a decade before that. The 2016–20 correlation was 0.47, and the 2018–20 was 0.55. Forty-eight percent of those who wanted to reduce immigration in 2016 no longer did in 2020 – 40% now felt current levels were acceptable and 8% wanted an increase. Forty-five percent of those who wanted an increase in 2016 no longer backed this in 2020, with a third now wanting to keep things the same and 12% now favoring a decrease. Forty-five percent of those who wanted to keep things the same in 2016 now either favored an increase (29%) or a decrease (16%). This movement wasn't fully random. In this case, unlike in 2006–10 where changes were closer to symmetric, it leaned heavily away from restriction: only 52% of those who wanted to reduce immigration in 2016 still did in 2020, but 85% of those who wanted the level preserved or higher continued to in 2020. This again puts a low upper bound on the level of nativism in the public, unless we assume that today's nativists are much

Immigration in the Court of Public Opinion

more prone to waffling and wavering than those in the past. We will return to the expansionist trend in opinion shortly, but for now the point is simply that people's attitudes about the proper level of immigration move around quite a bit, likely reflecting the ambivalence and mix of positive and negative considerations that the subject elicits for a majority of Americans.

Persuasion

It is one thing to show that opinions change, and something else to show that they change *systematically* in response to the same kinds of cues and persuasion techniques known to move opinion on other policy areas. Although several well-designed studies, such as that of Daniel Hopkins and colleagues,[12] have established that immigration attitudes are not responsive to the correction of widespread misperceptions about inflated numbers of immigrants and illegal immigrants living in the country, numerous other studies suggest that other stimuli do produce change. Opinions about immigration (including both illegal and legal immigration) do respond to cues from partisan leaders' position-taking.[13] Arguments that relate to core liberal values, such as equality, individualism and self-sufficiency, and the rule of law, also can shift opinions – a point we return to in the next chapter. There is also evidence that information about whether immigrants are learning English and integrating can boost support for increasing immigration.[14] So, too, can encouraging people to think about their own family's immigrant heritage[15] or to try to view the world through immigrants' eyes.[16]

Aggregate Change

If immigration attitudes are not fixed and are subject to persuasion, we should be able to find evidence of aggregate change in response to movement in the political and messaging environment. Eras of intensely anti-immigrant rhetoric should produce more support

Moderation, Malleability, and the Myth of Warring Camps

for restriction. Eras more friendly to immigration should see rising support for large-scale admission. As we showed in chapter 1, anti-immigration sentiment in the long-running Gallup time series on the level of immigration, which first asked the question in 1965, topped out in 1994, with 65% of Americans preferring less immigration and only 6% wanting more.[17] This was an era in which political rhetoric in both parties contended with immigration as a "fiscal burden," and leaders such as GOP runner-up for the 1990s presidential nomination Patrick Buchanan, Governors Pete Wilson of California and Lawton Chiles of Florida led the charge to restrict immigrants' access to public benefits and stop illegal immigration. National welfare reform in the mid-1990s responded to these concerns by limiting access to most federal welfare programs to legal immigrants who had been in the country at least five years. Even Democrats' rhetoric often sounded harsh notes about enforcing immigration law: Bill Clinton's mid-1990s State of the Union Addresses boasted of hitting targets for the arrest and deportation of illegal immigrants.

But as this rhetoric faded, so did the fervor for restriction. In fits and starts, including a brief spike after the 9/11 attacks, support for decreasing immigration has fallen by more than half, to 31% in 2021. Support for increasing immigration has increased five-fold from 6% to 33% and now just outstrips support for decreasing immigration – a situation that would have been unimaginable to those who wrote in the 1990s about the putative "disconnect" between sentiment for restricting immigration in the public and the expansionist character of immigration policy.[18] The rise in pro-immigrant sentiment since the mid-1990s is not just a "thermostatic" reaction to Trump. It unfolded over decades and through both Democratic and Republican administrations and has lasted well into the Biden administration.

To those accustomed to thinking of our own era as one suffused with nativism, it is perhaps puzzling that the rise in support for immigration not only continued but accelerated during the Trump years. One would especially not expect to find this to have occurred among Republicans. Yet, while support for reducing the level of immigration among Republicans jumped from 50%

Immigration in the Court of Public Opinion

in the 2012 ANES to 61% in 2016 at the end of Trump's first presidential campaign, it then dropped in 2020 to 44%. So, while recent years have seen disquieting instances of bluntly nativist discourse, they have also been marked by a full-throated rebuke of such rhetoric from much of the political establishment and many other opinion leaders in mass media and entertainment, including many Republicans. Trump himself wavered in his characterization of immigration, often praising immigrants and legal immigration, and sometimes even sympathizing with Dreamers. The broader context is one in which egalitarian values are on the rise, as seen in the dramatic rise of racial liberalism among whites and even, on some measures, among white conservatives. Immigration attitudes have moved in tandem.

Despite this momentum, the future direction of opinion about immigration is difficult, if not impossible, to predict. Events, crises, and unexpected changes in political mood have a habit of getting in the way of extrapolation. This uncertainty is itself part and parcel of what we have argued in this chapter. Americans' immigration attitudes are varied and complex, often ambivalent, and sometimes open to influence. This is true of the public as a whole and even among partisan segments of the public often assumed to have very strong and uniform hostility or sympathy toward immigrants. What accounts for these patterns, in the sense of their motivational foundations, is the focus of the next chapter.

3

Motivations

Americans tend to hold complex mixes of pro- and anti-immigration policy preferences. But why do people make decisions about immigration issues the way that they do? In this chapter, we survey the major theories about these motivations, which fall mainly into two species: *economic* and *cultural*. Economic theories imagine people as rational calculators of economic interest when they form opinions about immigration. Cultural theories focus on factors that go well beyond the financial bottom line. They consider how immigration attitudes are shaped by social identities and attachments, the values and norms of a society, and how well people believe immigrants will fit in. Among cultural theories we distinguish group-based motivations such as prejudice or favoritism for co-ethnics from values-based motivations such as a belief in equality or the rule of law.

After outlining these theories, we return to the American National Election Studies, first to explore how support for the claims of these competing perspectives has waxed and waned, and then to examine how well they account for Americans' preferences over which *types* of immigrants to admit and *on what terms*. In showing that liberal principles are more central to these choices than racial identities, we illustrate the importance of values in underpinning the tendency to hold a mix of pro-immigrant positions on some policies and restrictive positions on others.

41

Economic Motivations

The signal assumption behind the economic models is that people are motivated to maximize "utility" – which amounts to well-being. The link from utility-maximization to immigration attitudes occurs when people link immigration policies to economic gains and losses. In the narrowest sense, people care about immigration to the degree that they think it alters their wages, job prospects, the prices they pay at the supermarket, or the tax increases they might be expected to sustain, or that immigrants will "crowd out" the benefits to which natives might be entitled. Most straightforwardly, people oppose immigration when they assess its material costs to be greater than any expected benefits to them. This economic self-interest hypothesis has focused primarily on job threat, the belief that immigrants will take away jobs from low-wage workers, although fears of job loss or lower pay might also apply to high-skilled tech workers competing with engineers and software developers from China and India. On the other hand, people in secure occupations with money to spare might favor low-wage immigration, if they think that, as a result, they'll pay less for childcare, landscaping services, and the like.

Despite the folk wisdom that economic motives govern immigration attitudes, it is difficult to find dispositive and consistent evidence of this kind of thinking in the public at large. When asked directly, many Americans do express some concern about how immigration will affect their livelihoods. Workers without a college education, who tend to be most exposed and vulnerable to job or wage loss from competition with immigrants, express more opposition to immigration, as we saw in chapter 2. But it is unclear whether this is a result of personal job threat or the prevalence of anti-immigration attitudes such as prejudice against selected groups or chauvinism among this group. Some researchers have focused on the attitudes of small and specialized populations – for instance, the aforementioned native-born software engineer scrapping for a job at Google – and found that perceptions of an economic threat boosted hostility to immigration.[1] But

Motivations

most studies show that people do not reliably reject immigrants who would threaten their jobs.[2] For example, the concentration of immigrants in the industry that people work in – a gauge of whether they face meaningful wage and job competition – is only weakly related to preferences about immigration.[3] And insofar as exposure to higher tax burdens or exclusion from benefits are linked to immigration, the evidence of how this relates to policy preferences is at best inconsistent.[4] The evidence that economic self-interest is not paramount in most people's opinions about immigration is far from conclusive, but it has been enough to channel most research in other directions.[5]

A practical upshot of this is that alleviating opposition to immigration is not simply a matter of improving the economic security of the working class. If people were opposed to immigration primarily out of fears about its impact on their livelihoods, then strengthening the social safety net and job security or increasing wages would presumably defuse those concerns. However, even a basic gut check suggests that matters are far more complex. Chapter 5 below shows that opposition to immigration is considerably higher in Europe than in the US, despite the existence of more robust welfare states there. And while hostility to immigration increases with individual perceptions of a poor economy, there is at most a weak link between macroeconomic conditions and aggregate support for immigration.

What if we assume that people think beyond their own pocketbook and are concerned about the financial well-being of the broader community? They may care about the impact of immigration on the national economy because they believe that a strong economy will in the long run personally benefit themselves and those close to them – still a form of self-interest. Or they may be selflessly committed to wanting their country to thrive. Either way, this extension of economic motivation holds that people resent immigration if they believe that immigrants "take out" more in government services than they "put in" through taxes, *regardless of whether they themselves will see immediate benefit or harm*. We will term this kind of economic thinking "societal." There is quite a lot of evidence that people seem motivated by it in their political behavior. For example, Jens Hainmueller and Daniel Hopkins demonstrate a wide-ranging "hidden consensus" over an immigrant admissions policy favoring those who work hard, speak English, and (if at all possible) hold an advanced degree in a STEM field, regardless of where they come from.[6] The idea is that these immigrants will benefit the economy as a whole rather than being a threat to jobs or a drain on the public purse.

An implication of societal thinking is that people will tend to support "merit-based" immigration reforms that substitute highly skilled for less skilled newcomers. As discussed in chapter 1, among wealthy democracies, the US system is uniquely tilted toward family-based admissions. Only about 15% of all US Green Cards are awarded based on labor market skills, while over two-thirds are given based on family ties to US citizens or permanent residents. Most other nations rely heavily on criteria that signal ability to contribute economically and low likelihood of dependency, including educational attainment, job experience, proficiency in the native language(s), and even age. Commonly cited examples are the Canadian and Australian "points systems," which award points to prospective migrants based on each of these exacting criteria and more. Proponents of this kind of reform to the US system tout societal arguments, while opponents amplify the centrality of family unity in American values and attack the idea of importing just the world's elites as antithetical to the nation's traditional belief that anyone can come here, regardless of background, and succeed in the fertile soil of freedom.

Cultural Explanations

People are social animals embedded in a political community and invested in its integrity. They don't just want their country's *economy* to flourish, they also want to preserve its unique *national identity*. An enormous body of research is centered on the notion that concerns over "cultural threat" – broadly construed as fear about the survival of the dominant native group's status and norms – cause people to oppose immigration.[7] The argument is

Motivations

simple: insofar as immigrants are seen as people who do not fit a prevailing notion of "us" or who "we" are, they are deemed a potential threat to "our" identity and hostility toward them ensues. This kind of anxiety fuels demands for the assimilation of immigrants. One difficulty with this proposition, however, is that "cultural" notions of community turn out, much like the idea of "utility," to be extremely broad. As a result, there is real ambiguity about what is at the heart of so-called "cultural threat." We do not fully enter this morass, but simply center our analysis on two dimensions of culture: the social *groups* with which people identify, and the *values* by which they want to live.

When it comes to *groups*, the pre-eminent reference in contemporary scholarship is to ethnicity, which sometimes includes religion, and race. The group-centric perspective adopted in most research explains anti-immigrant hostility as follows: the native population has a strong sense of group identity, and it senses that immigrants imperil the status of this identity in some way. Typically, whites, sometimes referred to as "Euro-Americans," are the group viewed as defending their dominant values and position in a social hierarchy. There is a permanent struggle for hegemony of whites against a growing number of minorities, constantly replenished by immigration. The familiar references to "white nationalism" and "white backlash" are distillations of this argument.[8] A slightly different take is that anti-immigrant people are just motivated by simple prejudice, negative feelings directed at specific target out-groups such as Hispanics or Muslims or at a broad range of ethno-racial "outsiders" as a manifestation of ethnocentrism.[9]

The group-centrist view has predominated in academic research and much public commentary on immigration. Take, for example, *Washington Post* columnist Jennifer Rubin's summation of those who prefer less immigration: "Anti-immigration sentiment that Trump rode to the White House and stokes as a means of fueling his base's anger is not based on economic or other data. Strip away the fallacious arguments, and you arrive at an uncomfortable truth: This is largely about plain old bigotry."[10] Setting aside the dubious assertion that Trump actually rode anger about

Immigration in the Court of Public Opinion

immigration to the White House rather than prevailing in the general election in spite of his immigration stances (see chapter 2), the claim here is that opposition to immigration is grounded in racism even as it is couched in socially acceptable arguments. In this view, whites oppose immigration because they see whiteness as fundamental to what it means to be an American or because they have been carefully taught to dislike some or all non-whites.

In a society more than fifty years removed from the triumphs of the civil rights era, the group-centric view is dismal. It suggests that age-old notions of racial hierarchy persist in broad swaths of the public and continue to dominate their political attitudes and choices. It also holds out little hope for meaningful public debate about immigration. Persuasive efforts are futile when people's opinions are moored in tribal loyalties and hatreds. Advocates of this version of group-centrism understand arguments about immigration invoking economic interests or values as efforts to shroud disreputable motivations behind a cloak of respectability.

An important rival cultural interpretation emphasizes the values and norms that bind the political community over the parochial groups that populate it. There is in effect an assumed social contract, one that includes both our own notions about how we ought to treat people and our beliefs about how members of the community ought to behave. As this applies to immigration, people are assumed to be motivated by what they think is fair for immigrants, rather than whether they identify immigrants as part of "us" or part of "them" in an ethno-racial or ideological sense. Fairness judgments are rendered based on whether a policy (or an immigrant who may benefit from a policy) strikes people as consonant with their understanding of what immigrants owe their adoptive political community and what it owes them in return.

Many of these beliefs are bound up with questions about assimilation, which (in turn) engage bedrock beliefs about egalitarianism, legalism, and individualism.[11] In this view, measures of commitment to abstract and universalistic values will be strongly tied to opinions about immigration, and they will often override feelings of ethnic prejudice or solidarity. Accordingly, as we will show below, support for different immigration policies varies

46

Motivations

depending on the salience of frames, information, and policy details that accentuate certain values and de-emphasize others. The values-centric view can best explain why people hold the varied opinions about immigration that they do, even about policies that are closely tied to a single ethnic group. For example, if hostility toward Hispanics were the major motivation in Americans' attitudes about illegal immigration, we would struggle to explain why so many people support *both* stepped-up enforcement of immigration law *and* a pathway to citizenship for a group of immigrants that widely elicits a mix of sympathy and threat.

The Evidence

For a broad overview of how the various theories have fared over time, with as close to an apples-to-apples comparison as possible, we return to the American National Election Studies (ANES). These surveys have reliably measured Americans' preferences about desired immigration level for decades, and they have also included reasonable proxies for economic, group-centrist, and values-based motivations. The main weakness of the ANES is that it includes a large collection of identity-related measures but few that tap into core values. For example, despite its centrality in the American political tradition, individualism has not been measured on the ANES since the early 1990s. Nor has humanitarianism been measured in nearly twenty years. There are also not enough ethnic minority respondents to look at trends over time separately by race and ethnicity.

The longest-serving consistent measure of immigration policy preference is the ubiquitous question the ANES has asked in most of its surveys since 1992 and which we have discussed in chapters 1 and 2: "Do you think the number of immigrants from foreign countries who are permitted to come to the United States to live should be increased a little, increased a lot, decreased a little, decreased a lot, or left the same as it is now?" Our goal in this section is to explain why people take one position on this question versus another.

47

Immigration in the Court of Public Opinion

How should we measure people's economic self-interest? One way would be to simply ask them whether they thought that immigration took jobs from or lowered the wages of native-born Americans. While this simple approach is tempting it is usually eschewed for two reasons: 1) people do not reliably differentiate among various consequences of immigration on economics, culture, and crime, making it very difficult to see what is really motivating them; 2) there is too little difference between the supposed cause (perceived economic impact of immigration) and the supposed effect (a given attitude on immigration policy). Put differently, it is easy to demonstrate that thinking "immigrants are bad for the economy" is bound up with the belief that "immigrants cause crime" or the belief that "immigration should be reduced," but it is harder to know what to make of these inter-correlations.

To create a little more "distance" between these concepts, we use survey questions probing assessments of economic well-being that do not themselves refer to immigration, such as pessimism about the economy. This outlook arguably will boost opposition to immigration. The ANES has consistently measured the economic outlook of people both from an egocentric and a societal perspective, and both with respect to how people think about the past (retrospectively) or the future (prospectively). Here, we use four questions classified as indicated:

– "Would you say that you and your family are better off or worse off financially than you were a year ago?" (Self-interest, Retrospective).
– "Now looking ahead: do you think that a year from now you and your family will be better off financially or worse off, or just about the same as now?" (Self-interest, Prospective).
– "Would you say that over the past year the nation's economy has gotten better, stayed the same, or gotten worse?" (Societal, Retrospective).
– "What about the next twelve months? Do you expect the economy to get better, get worse, or stay about the same?" (Societal, Prospective).

What we want to know, in short, is how strongly and in which direction each version of "economic outlook" predicts people's

Motivations

desire to reduce immigration at various points in time. This can be expressed by a linear regression coefficient, which is nothing more than an attempt to express how much a dependent variable – in this case people's desired level of immigration – moves in response to a one-unit change in another variable, in this case feelings about the state of the personal or national economy.

Figure 3.1 maps out this relationship, as it exists for white American respondents, for every year in which all four types of questions were asked. If the dot is above the zero line in a given year, this means that (on average) more economic *optimism* yields a greater desire to *increase* immigration, as economic explanations suggest. If the dot is below the zero line, it means that more economic *pessimism* predicts more support for decreasing immigration. If the dot is close to zero, this means that knowing somebody's economic outlook tells us nothing about whether they want less or more immigration – that economic pessimists and optimists have roughly the same opinions about whether to increase or decrease immigration.

Two further points before proceeding with the evidence. First, each dot in Figure 3.1 has a line with spiked end points running through it, which represents statistical uncertainty about the true relationship between economic optimism and opinions about immigration. Longer lines mean more uncertainty. In cases where these vertical lines cross the horizontal zero line, there is too much uncertainty to say confidently that any true positive or negative relationship exists between economic optimism and opinion about immigration. Second, we look at these relationships in two ways. One graph looks at the simple, bivariate relationship between economic outlook and desired immigration level – whether economic optimists and pessimists have different views, on average, about immigration. The other looks at the *net* relationship between views of the economy and immigration opinions *after we hold constant various other important features of people's political views* – their ideology (running from extremely liberal to extremely conservative) and their party identification (running from strong Democrat to strong Republican). The idea is to see whether any simple relationships between economic outlook

Figure 3.1. Economic Outlook and Desired Immigration Level

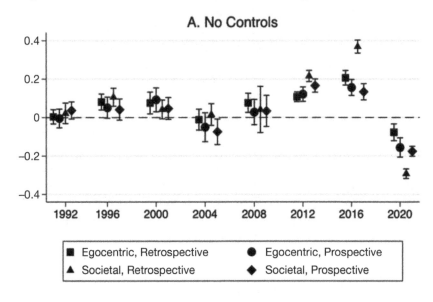

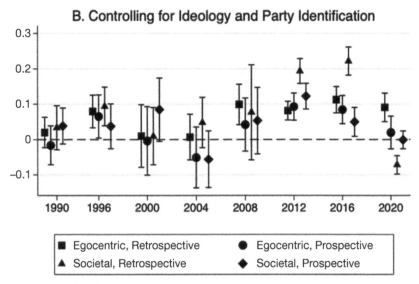

Source: ANES Cumulative, and ANES 2020 Time Series study

Motivations

and immigration level hold up even when we take account of and hold constant these other basic orientations to politics.

The takeaways from Figure 3.1 are relatively straightforward. The apparent relationship between broad economic assessments and desired immigration level bounce around somewhat but seem to have increased over the past couple of election cycles. The *direction* of the relationship is unstable and depends on who is the incumbent president. When the incumbent is a Republican, economic optimism is generally either unrelated or in a few cases negatively related to the desire to increase immigration; where the incumbent is a Democrat (Clinton or Obama), the relationship is strong and positive. This suggests to us that most of this relationship is more about basic political outlook than about economic assessments. People generally issue more positive assessments of the economy when their preferred party is in power, and as a result the connection may not *really* be about economics but about the relationship between partisanship and immigration attitudes that was articulated in the previous chapter. Sure enough, the relationships are much weaker in the bottom panel, when we control for basic political outlook. This suggests that beliefs about the economy, in and of themselves, aren't playing a strong independent role.

What about the group-centric view? A common practice in research on ethnocentrism and group prejudice is to use what the ANES calls "feeling thermometers," a measure of group affect that uses temperature as an analogy. Positive feelings are labelled "warm," with a maximum score of 100 degrees, and negative feelings are labelled "cold," with a minimum of 0. These questions have been consistently asked with reference to "Whites," "Hispanics," "Blacks," and "Asians" and in some studies to "immigrants" and "illegal immigrants" too. Theories of prejudice and ethnocentrism focus on people's *relative* feelings about their racial "in-group" versus out-groups. We adopt this approach in examining the influence of these group-centric motivations. Figure 3.2 maps the key relationships by year of survey – again, considering only white respondents and both with and without controlling, or holding constant, people's party identification

Immigration in the Court of Public Opinion

and ideology. Specifically, we look at whether warmer ratings of white people (the racial in-group in this case) and colder ratings of minority group members (the racial out-groups) predict less support for immigration. In all cases, a dot above the horizontal zero line means that *liking* that ethnic group translates into favoring *more* immigration, while a dot below the horizontal zero line means that liking that ethnic group translates into wanting less immigration. In all cases, the relationships shown control for attitudes toward each of the other groups. So, for instance, square dots represent the relationship between anti-Hispanic sentiment and opinion about immigration levels *net* of people's feelings about the other three groups – whites, blacks, and Asians. Put differently, we look at whether two white people who have the same feelings about whites, blacks, and Asians but different feelings about Hispanics also tend to register different views about whether to increase or decrease immigration. If prejudice against Hispanics *per se* is driving opposition to immigration, we should see the square dot fall below the horizontal zero line. If this relationship is strong enough for us to be confident about it, we should also see that the vertical line intersecting this square dot is fully below the zero line and does not cross it.

What seems apparent from Figure 3.2 is that whites who have more favorable feelings toward each racial out-group – Hispanics, Asians, and blacks – also tend to want to increase immigration, even controlling for how respondents feel about every other group. To the degree that anti-immigrant sentiment is out-group related, there isn't a single obvious group dominating the others; the effects of attitudes toward Hispanics have become slightly stronger over the last two elections (versus the other minority groups) but this is just a small difference. On the other hand, the large negative relationship between whites' feelings about other whites indicates that, all else being equal, expressing a high level of "warmth" for whites – net of how one feels about other groups – leads one to want reduced immigration.

One way of interpreting this is as evidence for ethnocentrism: in general, the more one prefers whites to a relatively undifferentiated conception of ethnic out-groups, the more one wants to

52

Figure 3.2. Group Prejudice and Desired Immigration Level

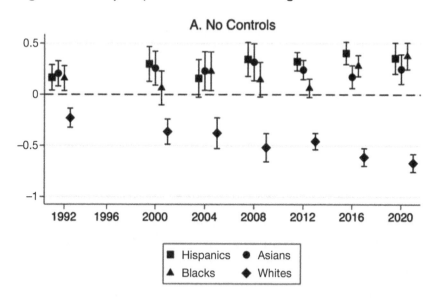

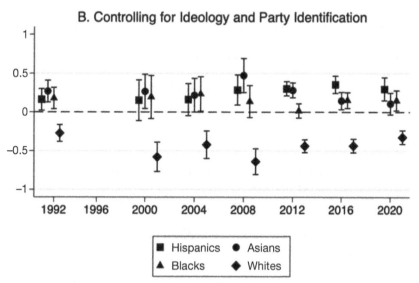

Source: ANES Cumulative, and ANES 2020 Time Series study

Immigration in the Court of Public Opinion

reduce immigration. None of this appears to change much either as years go by, or, for that matter, whether we decide to control for party identification and ideological orientation. This last point should not be lost in the shuffle: ethnocentrism overall has not gone up in the US public and may even have declined. Meanwhile, despite the ugly turn toward more overt discussion of race, national origin, and ethnicity in the nation's political rhetoric, ethnocentrism appears to play no greater role in promoting anti-immigrant sentiment now than it did before. And it is hardly surprising that people who say they have negative feelings toward non-white groups also tend to have negative attitudes about largely non-white immigrants.

Lastly, let us consider the role of values. Here, we are somewhat more constrained, to a single illustration, because the survey contains very few questions that tap the values people may associate with immigrants' rights and duties vis-à-vis what we might call the folk social contract. The only plausible indicator is the survey's egalitarianism battery, which includes the following six statements with which the respondent was asked to agree or disagree (coded here so that the most *egalitarian* answer receives the minimum score of 0, and the most *anti-egalitarian* answer receives the maximum score of 1):

- "We have gone too far pushing equal rights."
- "One of the big problems in this country is that we don't give everyone an equal chance."
- "Our society should do whatever is necessary to make sure that everyone has an equal opportunity to succeed."
- "It is not really that big a problem if some people have more of a chance in life than others."
- "The country would be better off if we worried less about how equal people are."
- "If people were treated more equally in this country, we would have many fewer problems."

Egalitarian values might be a source of support for more immigration for several reasons. They entail a strong belief in equality of opportunity and dislike of status differentials. This

54

Motivations

may make it harder for some individuals to accept the legitimacy of distinctions between insiders and outsiders. Especially when it comes to issues of illegal immigration and access to benefits and rights, egalitarians may bristle at the idea that there are second-class citizens in our midst. But even when it comes to the issue of how many should be allowed in, egalitarians may see immigration as the way to level opportunities between a relatively wealthy, powerful native population and often poor newcomers seeking a better life.

As with the previous figures in this chapter, Figure 3.3 maps out the relationship between these attitudes and the respondents' desired immigration level. In every case, a dot above the zero line means that pro-egalitarian sentiment predicts a desire for more immigration, a dot below indicates that pro-egalitarian sentiment predicts a desire for less immigration, and a dot around zero indicates that there is no relationship between support for equality and opinion about immigration.

Looking across items, in most cases, egalitarian responses predict a desire to increase immigration. This is especially so with respect to the "we've gone too far pushing equal rights" and "we should worry less about equality" questions and not so strongly with the "it's not a big problem if some people have more of a chance in life than others." The clear relationship between egalitarianism and support for more immigration has notably strengthened over the past three election cycles, notwithstanding the minor differences across individual items and the slight weakening of the relationships after controls for party identification and ideological self-placement.

Caveats

Having looked over the past three decades of ANES surveys, we've shown evidence consistent with all three of the main motivators we outlined at the beginning of this chapter, although the evidence for economic thinking is weak versus the other motivations. People tend to be wary of immigration when they are pessimistic about their (or the country's) economic situation,

Figure 3.3. Egalitarianism and Desired Immigration Level

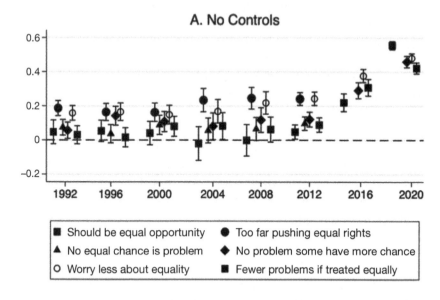

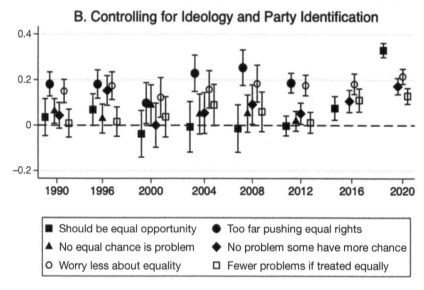

Source: ANES Cumulative, and ANES 2020 Time Series study

Motivations

when they view other racial or ethnic groups more negatively than their own, and when they express strong anti-egalitarian tendencies.

But there are three important limitations to the analysis so far. One is that it focuses only on the level of immigration question and therefore cannot tell us anything about why many people take pro-immigration positions on some policy issues and anti-immigration stances on others. Second, as we have noted, the ANES provides little in the way of measures of core values that are central to immigration debates – individualism, patriotism, the rule of law, and so on. The emphasis is heavily on indicators of identity and prejudice and, as befits an election survey, also economic indicators. Third, we have the familiar problem that correlation is not causation. Take, for example, the rather unsurprising fact that people who have cold feelings toward Latinos also are less supportive of immigration. Is this because prejudice drives opposition to immigration, opposition to illegal immigration spills over into prejudice against an ethnic group commonly conflated in the public discourse with illegal entrants, or because both prejudice and opposition to immigration are connected to some unmeasured conservative, conformist, or traditionalist orientation toward social change? We needn't single out group-centrism in this regard. Are egalitarians pro-immigrant because of their universalistic commitment to equal treatment, or is the egalitarianism measure essentially a proxy for low levels of racial prejudice – or even for "anti-racism"?

Improving the Evidence through Survey Experiments

One way to make progress in disentangling these motivations is to turn to experiments that we place inside surveys. These experiments use the power of randomization to get a better handle of which kinds of information and arguments influence voters' opinions. Voters are exposed at random to different versions of a policy question, with some of them being given only the question

Immigration in the Court of Public Opinion

itself and others being given certain information or arguments in addition to the question. If their answers differ, we can say with certainty that the active ingredient in the difference was the information we provided, since everything else in the setup is alike and the two groups of voters (those who receive the policy question with additional information and those who receive only the question) do not differ on average in any other way. We can then make educated guesses about which motivations are at work. If people seem to respond heavily to information about immigrants' ethnic background, that will point to group-centrism. If they respond minimally to race and ethnicity cues but are swayed more by information that signals core values such as self-sufficiency, equal treatment, or respect for the rule of law, that will point to societal or values-based motivations.

To illustrate, let's begin by focusing on what a simple experiment can tell us about the aspect of immigration policy we've considered throughout this chapter: how many immigrants people think should be allowed to come to the US. We showed, in Figures 3.1–3.3, that this attitude seems to move weakly in tandem with economic anxiety and more strongly with both a group-centrist tendency to rank one's own racial group over others and with core values (namely the degree to which one expresses "egalitarian sentiment"). How might we pinpoint the specific, causal role of one of these motivations, in a way that assuages some of the concerns about correlational evidence raised earlier?

In 2018, we ran our own survey, loosely based on the "level of immigration" question. Our interest was in explaining support for a hypothetical immigration policy we described as follows: "A non-partisan commission has recommended increasing the number of legal immigrants allowed to come to the United States from Mexico each year by 100,000." Respondents were, at random, either given *only* this description *or* assigned to read this description appended with one of the following:

– "Critics of the proposal say that these immigrants might take jobs from Americans or use welfare." [The *One-Sided Negative* condition.]
– "In order to be admitted, these immigrants would have to agree

Motivations

to work, support themselves financially, and learn English." [The *Functional Assimilation* condition.]

– "... to protect innocent people whose lives are threatened by violent drug cartels. In order to be admitted, these immigrants would have to demonstrate that their own safety or the safety of their families is in serious danger." [The *Refugee* condition.]

– "In order to be admitted, these immigrants would have to be sponsored by a sibling, parent, or adult son or daughter who is a US citizen. US citizens who legally sponsor their close relatives to immigrate to the US often wait more than ten years for them to receive a visa because of restrictions on annual immigration from each country. Supporters of the proposal say that we should reduce the amount of time that US citizens have to wait in order to be reunited with their families." [The *Family Reunification* condition.]

Here is why this setup is especially useful, as compared to the correlational data we showed earlier. First, the group identity of the immigrants in question is held constant. They are stipulated to be from Mexico, and this does not change across conditions. Second, the various conditions appended to the root policy description all cleanly cue different aspects of the *values* people bring to immigration policy. They want people to work hard and speak English (that is, to assimilate functionally); they have a humanitarian impulse to help people escaping persecution; and they want to help people reunite with their families. Critically, because people are exposed to one condition or the other *at random*, we can rule out both reciprocal causation and spurious correlation: random assignment ensures that all the treatment groups are alike in every possible way *except for the information they receive*, and there is no possibility that respondents' under-lying preconceptions about immigration could have influenced which version of the poll question people received.

In *Immigration and the American Ethos*, Morris Levy and Matthew Wright report the results of this analysis. What stands out first and foremost is that the most negative (restrictive) groups are those that either received no expository information or only the criticism that immigrants coming in under this program "might take jobs from Americans or use welfare." The fact that these two

59

groups are not especially different from each other suggests that most people have internalized this kind of thinking, such that making it explicit doesn't really change anything. On the other hand, just mentioning any of the other values-laden rationales – in effect either making a case for why the policy accords with people's values (the *Refugee* and *Family* conditions) or assuaging their doubts about whether the policy will open the country to norm violation (the *Functional Assimilation* condition) – strongly boosts support. What is more, they do so quite strongly when on their own, but they still work even when paired with the criticism about taking jobs and using welfare.

What do we learn from this kind of evidence? For one thing, we've seen the power of various values-based appeals in a way that is much richer than the limited exposition in Figure 3.3. This, in and of itself, is significant. But beyond that, we've done so in a way that gets past the standard criticisms levied against survey research: we know that the differences that emerge are not driven by the fact that people's judgments of "values stakes" go together with judgments about racial groups in society or about economic threat.

Which Types of Immigrants Do People Prefer, and Why?

We can make further progress toward teasing apart the motivations behind Americans' opinions about immigration policy by turning the focus to a different question. Instead of "how many," we examine "which types." Since there are always more people who wish to immigrate to the United States than the country's laws permit to come, much of the contemporary debate over immigration policy concerns not only the level of admissions but the criteria for selecting those who get in (or get to stay if they are already present unlawfully).

To get at public preferences about what kind of immigrant should be advantaged, we presented people with characteristics of individual immigrants or groups of immigrants and asked them

60

Motivations

to choose who should be admitted. An important feature of this inquiry is that it varies different attributes or personal characteristics of hypothetical immigrants simultaneously. As an example, we might ask some randomly selected groups of respondents to consider admission of 1) a hypothetical immigrant from Latin America who speaks fluent English; 2) a Latin American-origin immigrant who does not speak English; 3) a European immigrant who speaks fluent English; and 4) a European immigrant who does not speak English. In this kind of experiment, where two or more attributes are varied at once, we can compare the extent to which support for the immigrant is driven by national origin or ethnicity (European vs. Latino), holding English proficiency constant. *And* we can compare the extent to which support is driven by English proficiency, holding immigrants' national origin background constant. For example, do people prefer European to Latin American immigrants of any given level of English proficiency? Or do they mostly focus on English proficiency, preferring those who speak English to those who do not, regardless of their ethnic backgrounds. These comparisons help ascertain whether the public makes choices among types of immigrants primarily based upon the immigrants' putative ethnicity, level of assimilation, ability to contribute economically, and so on.

Beyond helping adjudicate between group-centric, values-centric, and economic motivations, the results from such experiments carry significant real-world implications for what they can tell us about the range of immigration policies the public would support. If people turn out to care mostly about immigrants' racial backgrounds, strongly preferring whites to non-whites, this suggests that the public would only support immigration reforms that seek to slow or reverse the current trajectory of demographic change. Although a return to explicit national origins quotas such as those enacted in the 1920s is not on the horizon, there are indirect means of achieving this goal.

However, if people turn out to care mostly about immigrants' propensity to assimilate linguistically and economically, this suggests that the public would support policies that preserve large-scale immigration *provided that these policies require or*

Immigration in the Court of Public Opinion

at least encourage and facilitate this type of integration. These assimilationist provisions could appear as criteria for legal admissions, qualifications that illegal immigrants must meet to qualify for legalization and a pathway to citizenship in a comprehensive immigration reform bill, or programs run by government or private organizations to facilitate immigrants' integration in either case. Similarly, if what people care most about is immigrants' human capital – their education, job skill, and age – this would align with societal interpretations of motivation and suggest that the public might favor a transition to a merit-based "points system."

To pursue these possibilities, we conducted a study in 2013 that queried on a sample of approximately 2,500 US adults fielded by Survey Sampling International. The specific approach we used is called "conjoint analysis," commonly used in marketing to determine which of several aspects of a given product consumers value more highly than others. In our experiment, two hypothetical immigrants are compared to one another. They are represented by a matrix that contains a discrete number of attributes. We varied the immigrants' English ability, national origin (a marker of ethnicity), religion, employment status, age, and educational attainment. Figure 3.4 Panel A shows what these side-by-side comparisons looked like, with placeholders for each attribute. Panel B shows the range of possible attributes within each category. So, for example, a respondent might have been confronted with a choice between one potential immigrant who speaks English fluently, is Mexican, Christian, employed, thirty years old, and has a college degree, and a second who speaks no English, is from Germany, not religious, unemployed, fifty years old, and with a high-school degree.

A very large number of immigrant profiles are possible in this experiment because all the attributes are assigned at random. In one version of the experiment, respondents were told that each hypothetical immigrant was an applicant for legal admission. They could choose whether to admit the first immigrant only, the second immigrant only, neither, or both, understanding that all immigrants were applying legally.[12] A second version told respondents that each profile described an illegal immigrant who

62

Motivations

might or might not be included in a legalization program. In a third version, respondents were told that the immigrant profiles represented people illegally in the country, who had been brought to the US as children ("Dreamers"), thus potentially absolving them of the moral responsibility for breaking the law. The respondent then chose whether either, neither, or both immigrant profiles should be given legal status or not. Each respondent in all three versions saw five immigrant pairs, thus evaluating ten immigrants in total.

Overall, while 45% of all legal immigrants were accepted for admission in our experiment, only 33% of illegal immigrants not specified to be Dreamers were, while respondents approved a right to stay for 45% of Dreamers. The reason for this difference is that about one third of the participants in this exercise rejected all illegal immigrant profiles they saw, regardless of the individual attributes. This body of "categorical" opponents of illegal immigration points to a rigid application of the principle that laws ought to be followed and enforced. This is a value judgment, not racial prejudice: those who judged categorically excluded all illegal immigrants regardless of national origin, including members of their own ethnic or racial groups. Support rebounded considerably for legalizing Dreamers. Categorical opposition here was lower by 11% compared to the illegal immigrant profiles. Applying one's commitment is softened when it comes to young illegal immigrants, who were brought to the US as children. The Dreamers arguably are not themselves responsible for having violated the law and are thus treated quite a bit more leniently.

How much did individual attributes matter to people? It turned out that the answer is similar across the different versions of the experiment. That is, people prefer similar types of legal immigrants for admission and illegal immigrants for legalization. In the interest of space and simplicity, we therefore aggregate the results across all three versions of the experiment. As Table 3.1 shows, the main drivers of preferences for inclusion are indicators of linguistic assimilation and financial self-sufficiency. These are followed by an indicator of human capital – educational attainment – although age, a second metric commonly used in merit-based point systems,

Immigration in the Court of Public Opinion

Figure 3.4. Immigrant Profiles

Panel A: Format of Conjoint Experiment

Country of Origin	*origin1*	*origin2*
Language Skills	*lang1*	*lang2*
Education	*educ1*	*educ2*
Job History	*jobperf1*	*jobperf2*
Family	*family1*	*family2*
Age	*age1*	*age2*
Religious Background	*rel1*	*rel2*

Panel B: Immigrant Attributes Varied in Conjoint Experiment

Characteristic	Possible Attributes
Country of Origin (*origin1, origin2*)	Mexico
	Germany
	China
	Nigeria
	Pakistan
Language Skills (*lang1, lang2*)	Speaks fluent English
	Speaks only limited English
	Speaks no English
Education (*educ1, educ2*)	No high-school degree
	High-school degree but no college degree
	College degree
Job Performance (*jobperf1, jobperf2*)	Mostly employed for last five years
	Mostly unemployed for last five years
Age (*age1, age2*)	30
	40
	50
	60
	70
Religious Background (*rel1, rel2*)	Christian
	Muslim
	Not religious

Motivations

Table 3.1. Which Types of Immigrants Do People Prefer?

Comparison of Immigrant Types	Effect on Percentage Who Supported Admission / Legalization
Mostly employed vs. Mostly unemployed	+15
Fluent vs. No English	+17
Age 30 vs. Age 70	+3
College Grad vs. No High-School Degree	+10
Christian vs. Muslim	+10
German vs. Mexican	+2

is unimportant. Those of prime labor market age are only slightly preferred to those at or near retirement age.

Our results give scant support to group-centric theories based on ethnicity and race. German immigrants, a stand-in for Europeans, get only a very tiny edge over Mexican immigrants. We note also that Chinese immigrants were only one point less likely to get the nod than Germans, a virtual tie, though Nigerians and Pakistanis fared a few points worse. Moreover, it turns out that these results are virtually identical when we look only at white respondents, who were more than 70% of our sample. The fact that the public evinces only a minute preference for putatively white over Latino immigrants is striking given how much of the discourse about the mass politics of immigration takes the pre-eminence of white supremacy or prejudice virtually for granted. To be sure, in environments where people lack information about immigrants' assimilation and human capital, research shows that they often fall back on ethnic stereotypes to make choices. But when it comes to *motivations* the results here suggest that what matters to people largely are factors other than ethnicity. There is little here to suggest that race, *per se*, matters a whole lot compared to the other attributes we examined.

There is, on the other hand, evidence that religion counts in Americans' preferences over whom to admit or legalize.

Immigration in the Court of Public Opinion

People prefer Christian immigrants over non-religious ones (by approximately 5 points, not shown) and have a larger 10-point preference for Christians relative to Muslims. Religiosity and public affirmations of religious identity and conviction are much more prominent in US political culture than in other developed nations. Religion – and in particular Christianity or, post-World War II, "Judeo-Christian heritage" – remains a component of many people's conception of what it means to be an American. And the common stereotypic conflation of Islam with terrorism, accentuated following the 9/11 attacks, further serves to stigmatize would-be Muslim immigrants. On the one hand, since Muslims make up a small percentage of all US immigrants, prejudice against them can't be a factor in most people's reactions to most immigration policy issues. But the anti-Muslim bias shows that group-centric attitudes not strictly tied to ethnicity alone can matter. Indeed, it has been noted by many observers that some of the rhetoric surrounding Islam in the US bears an uncanny resemblance to the anti-Catholic nativist tracts of the mid-nineteenth century, which castigated Irish and German immigrants as unsuited for democratic citizenship.

The clearest implication of this conjoint experiment is that the public strongly prefers immigrants who assimilate linguistically and demonstrate sufficient potential integration into the economy to be self-sufficient, a result paralleled by the findings from the experiment detailed in the previous section. In order for a reform proposal to garner public support it seems it must ensure that beneficiaries would possess these attributes. The trouble in relation to illegal immigration is that such proposals also run up against the large minority of the public that staunchly opposes legalization on the grounds that it "rewards lawbreakers," evident in the categorical stances many of our respondents took toward illegal immigrants. In the court of public opinion, the tussle will hinge on whether arguments amplifying assimilationist demands or arguments emphasizing breach of the rule of law gain more traction.

The implications for the design of legal immigration policy are murkier. Although people prefer English-speaking immigrants and

Motivations

those with a job, this does not imply that they would prefer to screen for these qualities at the point of admission. Many of those who strongly believe these assimilationist attributes are important also would give immigrants a chance to integrate once they have arrived. If the US did adopt a points system, it is not clear how the desired "points" would be distributed. Would educational attainment count as much as or more than English-speaking? How much would occupational qualifications count?

There is little doubt that Americans, like citizens across the West, place a "premium" on highly skilled immigrants such as engineers over low-skilled immigrants. A Gallup poll conducted in January 2013 found 71% of Americans in support of "increasing the number of visas for legal immigrants who have advanced skills in technology and science," with only 27% opposed. Even here, there are limits. A United Technologies/National Journal Congressional Connection poll from later that year found that the plurality preference, when offered, was to keep the number of high-skilled foreigners who are eligible to live and work here the same (47%) rather than to increase (22%) or decrease (24%) it. And only 29% said the US should admit "as many high-skilled foreign workers as companies want to hire," while 61% said there should be "restrictions."

But it also is important to recognize that support for more highly skilled immigration does not necessarily mean that Americans strongly favor trading it off against family-based visas. Polling on these types of reforms has yielded inconsistent results, with many indicating weak support for sharply reducing family reunification.[13] A *New York Times*/CBS poll has asked "how should priority be given when admitting immigrants," offering a choice between prioritizing "people who have family members already living in the US" and allocating visas primarily "based on education, job skills, and work experience." In April 2007, it found a bare 51% majority support for prioritizing skills, with 34% favoring family. In 2013, the majority favoring skills grew to 58–27. But in the most recent iteration of the question, in May 2019, the split was only 48–40. A CNN poll conducted in September 2017 found a similar 51% majority saying that "job skills and education"

67

Immigration in the Court of Public Opinion

should be more important than "family members already living in the US" in deciding which immigrants to admit.

Yet a *Washington Post*/ABC poll conducted in May 2007, which asked whether priority should be given to "those who already have a brother, sister, parent, or grown child living here legally" versus "those who have no such relatives in the US but have skills and education that are in need here," found a much more even split. Thirty-five percent favored skills and 34% family, with 13% volunteering that both should get "preference" and 14% volunteering neither.[14] The *Post*'s question differs from the *Times*' in at least two key respects: it specifies that the ability of legal immigrants to bring over their relatives is at issue, whereas the *Times* and CNN refer only to "people already living here," and it refers to "skills and education" without using the positive valence of "jobs." But even the *Times* polls reveal nothing approaching an unalloyed consensus in favor of prioritizing skills over family unity, and the majority preference can erode with slight changes in question wording. Finally, some Americans also believe that a healthy economy needs more low-skilled workers willing to do jobs that American citizens disdain. A Bloomberg poll conducted February 15–18, 2013, found as much combined support for prioritizing visas for low-skilled workers "such as those in construction or hotel employees" (14%) or agricultural workers (15%) as for prioritizing high-skilled workers (29%).[15]

More recently, we asked respondents on a YouGov sample embedded in the 2015 Cooperative Congressional Election Survey whether they would support reallocating some family-based visas to highly skilled immigrants, reallocating some skills-based visas to family-based immigrants, or keeping things as they are. All respondents were informed that the US issues about 1 million Green Cards each year, and that almost seventy out of every 100 go to family reunification while fifteen out of every 100 are awarded based on job skills and employer need. Despite this information, support for reallocating visas toward skilled immigrants barely edged out the reverse option, 19% to 16%, while the great majority preferred to stay with the status quo.

Motivations

The totality of our findings about public opinion indicate that people prefer to admit immigrants with a high potential for successful integration into the economy and culture. To the extent that people weigh immigrants' ethnicity, the evidence suggests that it is used as an auxiliary stereotype rather than a criterion in itself. Whereas it has become fashionable for pro-immigrant politicians to deride those who favor assimilation or merit-based immigration as adopting race-neutral rhetoric to further the racist goal of whitening the immigrant stock, our results suggest precisely the opposite. Stereotyping is common, but relatively few Americans are motivated, at root, by concerns over racial composition. This suggests that a healthier and more substantive debate over immigration that elucidates policy specifics would reduce the power of stereotyping. This kind of discussion largely prevailed in the US for over thirty years following the 1965 Hart-Celler Act but has become a casualty of vitriolic partisan polarization – one of many forces that are stymying change.

Concluding Thoughts on Motivation

We have distinguished between economic and cultural theories regarding what motivates immigration attitudes, and further divided the latter category into theories based on group identity and status versus value orientations. Trend evidence collected by the ANES gives some support to all three interpretations of opinions on the proper level of immigration without indicating the relative strength of each motive or the conditions under which they are salient. In going beyond the correlational data to survey experiments that tried to isolate a causal role for political beliefs, we found stronger evidence for the role of value-based appeals to the abilities and predicament of immigrants in determining a willingness to admit more.

Survey experiments gave us a better handle on which school of thought best explains Americans' preferences for certain *types* of immigrants and, relatedly, why individuals' opinions so often differ across different areas of immigration policy – the pattern of

Immigration in the Court of Public Opinion

complexity and ambivalence outlined in chapter 2. What makes many people who want less immigration, or at least no more, support a path to citizenship for millions of illegal immigrants? What, on the other hand, makes a sizable portion of the public receptive to immigration but opposed to – often dead-set against – an amnesty for immigrants living in the country without legal status? Why do some Americans favor rebalancing legal admissions toward skills-based immigration while others favor the continuation of a predominantly family-based admissions regime?

When group-based and values-based theories are pitted against one another experimentally as potential answers to these questions, the evidence for values-based motivations is strong and the evidence for explanations rooted in ethnic prejudice and solidarity or economic self-interest weak. This obviously does not mean that prejudice and pocketbook concerns play no role in shaping attitudes about immigration. But it does indicate that much of the commentary about why Americans support or oppose immigration sells the public short. The values that people invoke in debates over immigration are often sincerely held. And when people are put to the test by policy questions that pit selfish or prejudicial motives against liberal values, it is these values that tend to win out.

American mass opinion about immigration does not hew reliably to the understanding of "liberalism" commonly found in encyclicals handed down from the ivory tower on the moral philosophy of whether it is permissible to restrict immigration at all. But it does conform remarkably well to what might be termed a folk notion of liberalism – the idea that policies should be judged based on their adherence to the values of individual liberty and responsibility, equal opportunity irrespective of circumstances of birth and background, and the rule of law. This is a far cry from the illiberal and angry outlook that so much elite commentary ascribes to the average citizen. The foundation of immigration attitudes on widely held values refutes the notion that a large segment of the American public is suffused with the nativist mindset that immigrants will constitute an irredeemably foreign minority that erodes America's national identity.

4

Assimilation Then and Now

The story of immigrant absorption is as old as America itself. By bringing strangers into "our" land, large-scale immigration has always raised fears about social cohesion and cultural unity. Will immigrants be loyal to their new country? Will they learn our language, adopt our values, and celebrate our holidays? In short, will "they" become more like "us," and how do we make sure this comes about?

In addressing these questions today, scholars and politicians focus on whether the trajectory of the Hispanic and Asian immigrants who have transformed the makeup of the United States will follow the pattern of their European predecessors. The historical concern that ethnic diversity threatens national unity appears more salient in the wake of the increased assertiveness about group identities triggered by the success of the civil rights movement. As long ago as 1971, Nathan Glazer and Daniel Moynihan wrote that the renewed emphasis on the value of "difference" had crushed the "liberal expectancy" that economic modernization would overcome the divisiveness of ethnic ties.[1] Instead, "identity politics" and "tribalism" now are dominant characterizations of American politics, with many commentators worrying that the old ideal of *e pluribus unum* sustained by assimilation is no longer viable.

Writers addressing the consequences of immigration for the country's future can be divided into two camps: the gloomy Cassandras who worry about the creation of a balkanized nation and the sanguine Pollyannas who say we've been here before, and

71

that today's immigrants will become Americanized just as previous newcomers had.[2] There are also multiculturalists whose worry is that assimilation will indeed proceed apace, the opposite concern of those who worry that immigrants are not adapting to America and adopting its traditions and beliefs. A lightning rod in this debate is Samuel Huntington's *Who Are We? The Challenges to America's National Identity*.[3] Huntington leaned toward the Cassandra end of the continuum and branded Hispanic immigration in particular as a serious threat to an American identity which he defined as a fusion of a democratic political creed and an "Anglo-Protestant" culture based on English, religiosity, and a strong work ethic. In less sophisticated terms, this animus toward immigration from Mexico surfaced in the Trump administration and in the views of his immigration guru, Stephen Miller.

Huntington maintained that the sheer extent of continuing immigration from Latin America, especially from Mexico, and high birth rates among Hispanics who share a language and religion and who are concentrated in the southwest of the United States close to their country of origin, means that they will not assimilate as had their European predecessors or as will their Asian contemporaries. The incentive to assimilate is further diminished by the rise of identity politics and multiculturalism's rejection of individualism in the name of a group's right to preserve its own culture. Finally, the growing adherence of bureaucratic, business, and intellectual elites to cosmopolitan values downplaying the significance of national loyalty and traditional patriotism has blurred the traditional definition of dominant beliefs that were the supposed end state of assimilation. We do not dismiss these challenges to national unity; rather we review the evidence of public opinion to assess the extent of old-style assimilation among Hispanic and Asian immigrants and to explore what the native mainstream expects of them.

What is Assimilation?

To assimilate is to become similar to. This leaves open the questions of who is becoming similar to whom, with regard to

Assimilation Then and Now

what, and whether assimilation is voluntary or coercive. In the context of immigration, assimilation means the creation of greater uniformity in society through the attenuation of ethnic differences. Change can be in more than one direction, of course, and one image of the American melting pot holds that its content evolves as new words become part of the common lexicon and new traditions penetrate the larger society. However, the dominant model of assimilation that emerged in the nineteenth century, and the one Huntington prefers, emphasizes a one-way movement toward the "Americanization" of immigrants.

By any definition, assimilation is a process that occurs over time, as immigrants and their offspring are exposed to and take on the dominant habits of their new country. The conventional "straight-line" hypothesis regarding change predicts that successive immigrant generations, whatever their national origin, will increasingly resemble each other, as they all become similar to the native-born Americans of European origin who are the presumed carriers of mainstream values.[4] Accordingly, third-generation immigrants – native-born residents with native-born parents – should be more similar to native-born whites than are the foreign-born from the same country.

Milton Gordon's seminal *Assimilation in American Life* (1964) distinguished between *structural assimilation* – involving the large-scale entry of native minorities and immigrants into the economic, social, and political institutions of the "host" society, ultimately leading to intermarriage with members of the ethnic core – and *cultural assimilation*, or the acquiring of a sense of common peoplehood through the adoption of the dominant values and customs.[5] In the political domain which is our focus, cultural assimilation meant, at a minimum, learning English, endorsing the national creed of democracy, equality, and individualism, and identifying oneself as an American.[6] Gordon was aware of the growing political demands for maintaining one's ethnic identity but posited that over time successive immigrant generations inevitably would forsake their ancestral language and customs; he did not envisage assimilation as a two-way street.

Immigration in the Court of Public Opinion

Most scholars agree that this model fits the path of the various European immigrant groups. Thanks in part to the inclusionary experience of World War II and the economic boom in its aftermath, the third generation of Emma Lazarus's "huddled masses" had become almost fully integrated into the white middle-class mainstream.[7] Upward mobility, residential integration, and intermarriage steadily grew. As for self-identification, when asked about their background people of European origin might refer to themselves as Italian-, Irish-, or Greek-American, but psychologically the emphasis would be on the national term after the hyphen. Their ethnic identification had become largely symbolic, a nostalgic attachment to the traditions of the old country that could be felt or occasionally displayed, as on St. Patrick's Day, without being incorporated into daily practice or imposing the social cost of being thought "un-American."[8]

More recent scholarship has questioned the applicability of Gordon's "straight-line" account for the experience of Hispanic and Asian immigrants. Alejandro Portes and his colleagues argue that technological change has created a new economy that makes structural assimilation a slow and bumpier road for less highly educated, principally Hispanic immigrant groups. The result is "segmented assimilation," with a subset of second-generation immigrants rejecting the mainstream values of self-reliance and educational achievement and becoming part of a non-white "underclass" rather than the mainstream.[9] Edward Telles and Christina Sue show evidence of the durability rather than a fading away of ethnic identification among Mexican Americans, though much other work has convincingly shown that these worries are at least overblown.[10] Finally, Richard Alba and Victor Nee modify Gordon's account, holding that mainstream culture – the supposed end point of assimilation – changes as immigrants add new ingredients to America's cultural mix. In this view, for immigrants, assimilation means movement toward a dominant set of values rather than complete absorption; for the mainstream, it means accepting new words, foods, music, and holidays.[11]

Assimilation Then and Now

Three Ideological Perspectives

Nativists would rather have fewer immigrants around in the first place. But for those already inside the gates, they assume that cultural differences between natives and immigrants are too large and deeply ingrained to be left alone. Even if immigrants are willing and able to blend in – and nativists tend to assume they are not – their cultural distinctiveness poses an acute threat to the nation's way of life. Thus, to the extent that immigrants are brought in at all, nativists demand heavy-handed programs of "Americanization," sponsored and run by government or "patriotic groups," using means that range from outright coercion to social pressure and invasive monitoring, to paternalistic hectoring, all alongside the more benign means of exhortation and education.

A more common view in American history is that immigration is desirable provided that immigrants blend in, and that immigrants are capable of doing so if they receive proper encouragement. This is the liberal view of assimilation – that the American way of life is in principle open to anyone, not to say everyone, irrespective of the circumstances of birth and background. Liberal assimilation can be monistic or pluralistic, with many points along the spectrum between the two. In the monistic view, which often prevailed before the mid-twentieth century but has fallen into disrepute among many of today's intellectuals and opinion leaders, assimilation is a process of cleansing. It means washing away all features of minority cultures; immigrants' speech, hygiene, manners, and political identification must change. In 1919, Theodore Roosevelt wrote that, to be treated as an equal, the immigrant must become "in every facet an American, and nothing but an American ... there can be no divided allegiance here. We have room for but one flag, the American flag. We have room for but one language here, and it is the English language ... and we have room for one sole loyalty and that is a loyalty to the American people."[12] This maximalist version of assimilation is exacting, and it can at times flirt with nativism when the slow pace of integration arouses

75

Immigration in the Court of Public Opinion

fears that the immigrants of today don't have what it takes or are remaining perpetually foreign. Especially under conditions of domestic instability or foreign threat, this anxiety can veer into illiberal demands for coercive assimilation programs aimed at a monoculture.

The current version of liberal assimilation is pluralistic rather than monistic. It interprets the melting pot as a process of blending not cleansing. Becoming American does not involve giving up every vestige of your origins. Calling oneself a hyphenated-American is acceptable, provided that the national identity after the hyphen has primacy. America enters a kind of contract with immigrants in which allegiance to the democratic creed, patriotism, self-reliance, and learning English goes along with the *voluntary* maintenance of ethnic cultures. Assimilation as articulated by liberalism does not require celebrating the same holidays, eating the same food, or giving up membership in ethnic organizations. Over the course of the twentieth century, assimilationist ideals were thinned out. American political, social, and commercial rhetoric now endorses a laissez-faire liberal ideal that not only gives immigrants the leeway to be ethnic but prizes ethnic heritage and diversity as being as American as apple pie.

To some, the private tolerance and valuation of difference isn't enough. Multiculturalists reject the contemporary liberal approach to assimilation as merely one more insidious form of coercion. Although no one is forced to surrender ancestral culture, immigrants are implicitly faced with a choice between blending in or remaining permanently outside the nation's mainstream. Multiculturalism not only gives one's "original" culture a pride of place in America – contemporary liberal assimilation does that too – it also views any impetus toward the adoption of majority norms and customs with suspicion. To guard immigrants against the ostensibly oppressive forces of conformity in a "post-colonial" society, multiculturalists demand special group-based protections, rights, and subsidies.

Giving the value of a common national identity short shrift, multiculturalism emphasizes the overweening psychological signif-icance of ethnic identity and calls on the government to advance

Assimilation Then and Now

the interests and standing of minority groups. Minority *cultures*, rather than simply minority *individuals*, should have equal rights and the government should act to preserve them. So, whereas nativists demand that government and civil society take coercive and invasive measures to preserve an Anglo-Saxon monoculture, multiculturalists advocate government intervention to preserve a purist version of ethnic monocultures and shield them from the incursion and taint of majority folkways. Though multiculturalism and nativism obviously differ in many ways, both reject Milton Gordon's assumption that over time assimilation would ultimately make ethnic identity an optional attachment. And both demand government intervention to protect the integrity of what they regard as sacrosanct groups.

In practice, the immigrant experience has not followed the nativist script. Immigrants have learned English, adopted the prevailing manners, and even changed their names to fit in and get ahead. At the same time, assimilation has tended to erode ethnic attachments and ancestral customs only over generations and less so within individual immigrants' own lives – especially those who arrive at an advanced age. Ethnic affinities retain their hold to varying degrees for several generations, and are routinely used to mobilize support for minority candidates and causes.[13] Immigration also has resulted in the evolution and expansion of mainstream popular culture. Pizza, sushi, and bagels have become part of the national cuisine; Yiddish words like chutzpah are part of the vernacular; karaoke is a common form of entertainment throughout the country; Ethnic Heritage months are part of the calendar and provide a temporal focus for entertainment and education. Grocery stores in cities with large immigrant populations have Hispanic and Asian aisles. Baseball, the national pastime, has followed suit in its marketing. On June 13, 2021, the Arizona Diamondbacks unveiled a new uniform referencing the Sonoran Desert and the state's Hispanic culture and planned to wear it on "Hispanic Heritage Weekend."[14] To date, fan reaction has been overwhelmingly positive. "Thin" assimilation is compatible with what might be called "festival" multiculturalism – the embrace of fusion cuisine, K-Pop, Kwanzaa, and Cinco de

Immigration in the Court of Public Opinion

Mayo. But this is a far cry from endorsing political multiculturalism's demand for group rights.

Despite warnings that "hard" multiculturalism will "disunite America" and cause "the twilight of common dreams," this perspective has achieved a remarkable rhetorical ascendancy in elite circles and has made small inroads into some corners of American electoral politics. Multiculturalism now is entrenched as an alternative civic religion to the liberal tradition that dominated until the 1960s. When Nathan Glazer wrote *We Are All Multiculturalists Now* in 1998, he was acknowledging the institutionalization of ethnic identity and group representation in academia and elsewhere. Glazer's main concern was the nation's special obligation to blacks, but he worried that multiculturalist policies could undermine the assimilation of immigrants and, derivatively, their commitment to a shared national identity.

The oft-expressed concern about immigrants' attitude toward America is a useful starting point for this chapter's analysis of the paths taken by successive generations of both Hispanic and Asian immigrants and the relative degree of acceptance of the nativist, liberal, and multiculturalist perspectives in public opinion. The aspect of "assimilation to what" addressed here is limited to the degree of adherence to those values and behaviors that define the historically dominant conception of what it means to be an American: a primary self-identification as an American rather than a member of an ethnic or racial group, patriotism, belief in the importance of learning English, and opinions about the value of minorities holding on to their distinctive customs.

In mining the available data, we concentrate on surveys with enough Hispanic and Asian respondents and measures of immigrant generation. Following standard definitions, the first generation are foreign-born, the second generation are those with at least one parent born abroad, and the third and subsequent generations are those born in the United States with two American-born parents. We principally rely on the American National Election Studies of 2016 and 2020, the Pew Latino National Survey of 2015, and the Cato Institute's Immigration and Identity Survey conducted in 2021 after Biden's assumption of the presidency. The ANES

78

Assimilation Then and Now

studies include only US citizens as respondents, so the first-generation immigrants in those samples have taken a step toward assimilation through naturalization. The Cato survey includes foreign-born respondents who are not American citizens.

Are Immigrants Assimilating?

Two Pew Research Center surveys conducted between late 2015 and early 2016 provide an important look at trends in Hispanic self-identification.[15] The authors cite the rising rate of intermarriage among Hispanics in the United States, with the result that the share of immigrants saying they have a non-Latino spouse (the term used by Pew) rises from 18% in the first generation to 65% in the third or higher generation of self-identified Hispanic adults.[16] Intermarriage is the most definitive indicator of assimilation, with implications for how ethnicity is defined and for America's sense of its own identity.

When asked by Pew how they identify or describe themselves, respondents could choose their family's country of origin, the pan-ethnic Hispanic or Latino term, or call themselves "American." The use of country of origin or Hispanic fell sharply as one moved from the first to the third generation; in contrast, self-identification as an American rose from 7% to 56% among the third or higher generation. Strikingly, among the 40 million Americans whom government surveys show as having Hispanic ancestry by self-report, 11%, mainly from later generations, did not identify themselves as Hispanic. This conforms to the straight-line model of assimilation predicting strong ties to an American national identity among later generations. Only 36% of foreign-born Hispanics said they consider themselves a typical American, a share that rose to 63% among the second generation and 73% among third or higher generations. Clearly, birth in the United States and a longer family history here makes seeing oneself as an American more natural and common.

The Pew report provides other evidence of the straight-line model. Language use changes across the generations, with fully

79

75% of the third generation saying that they mainly use English at home and just 24% saying they are bilingual. Across the generations too, connections to the home country decline, conversations with parents about their original cultures are less frequent, and friendship patterns become more diverse, all indicators of ongoing cultural integration.

A central issue in the debate over assimilation is whether immigrants come to identify as Americans. Because people have multiple identities, including ethnic and national identities, the question of primacy arises; recall Theodore Roosevelt's warning against immigrants' adopting a hyphenated identity implying dual loyalties.

The subjective problem of prioritizing one "we" over the other can arise when choices push in different directions. Assimilationists of both nativist and liberal persuasions assume that national loyalty will trump ethnic identification when these situations occur, as they did for Japanese Americans after Pearl Harbor. Below, then, we will consider the following questions: How do Americans, and immigrant groups in particular, balance their national and ethnic attachments? Are these identifications complementary, in the sense of going together, or do they collide, with a strong sense of ethnic consciousness eroding feelings of belonging to the country as a whole? How do people order their dual identities? And do these choices vary across the country's main ethnic groups and across immigrant generations along the lines proposed in the assimilation model? To get at identification with alternative communities, a common approach is to ask people *separately* about the importance of their race or ethnicity and of being an American to their personal identity. This allows comparison of identity choices across ethnic groups and immigrant generations. The assimilation model assumes that ethnicity will fade among immigrants over time, while seeing oneself primarily as "just an American" will become more prevalent.

Here we present the relevant data from three recent studies: The ANES studies of 2016 and 2020 and the Cato Institute 2021 Immigration and Identity Survey.[17] As studies of presidential voting, the ANES surveys included only naturalized citizens; one

Assimilation Then and Now

advantage of the Cato survey is that its sample of foreign-born (first-generation) immigrants includes noncitizens as well. Figure 4.1 shows the proportions of each of the country's four main ethnic groups saying that their ethnic and American identities are either "extremely" or "very" important to them, a relatively strong test of group consciousness.

The results are quite consistent across all three surveys. Ethnic group identity is weakest among whites, ranging from just 20% in the 2020 ANES to 31% in the Cato survey. The personal importance of American identity declined between 2016 and 2021, among whites most clearly but also in minority ethnic groups. This may reflect the polarizing impact of Trump's Make America Great Again slogan and the emergence of nationalism as a dirty word in media coverage of politics. Ethnic identification is consistently strongest among blacks, with Hispanics and Asians falling in between but closer to blacks in the extensiveness of a strong sense of ethnic attachment.

Among whites, the importance of being an American dwarfs a strong attachment to one's ethnic group. It is significant, though, that identification as an American is almost as strong among the three minority groups as their ethnic identification. Blacks express a quite similar sense of attachment to being black and American, a clear indication of the "double consciousness" that W.E.B. Dubois saw as the essence of black experience in America.[18] For example, in the 2020 ANES survey, 80% of blacks said their racial identity was extremely or very important to them, while 72% said this about being American.

The evidence that ethnic identification is durable among the Hispanic and Asian groups made up of more recent immigrants might be viewed as fuel for nativist anxieties about dual loyalties. However, the data in Figure 4.1 do not speak directly either to change across successive generations or to the prioritization of identity choice. They do, however, show that in general ethnic and American identities do not collide. Strong ethnic and national attachments go *together*, as measured by a familiar statistical tool, the correlation coefficient. In the 2020 ANES study, the correlations are 0.40 for whites, 0.36 for blacks, 0.27 for

Immigration in the Court of Public Opinion

Figure 4.1. The Personal Importance of Ethnic and American Identities

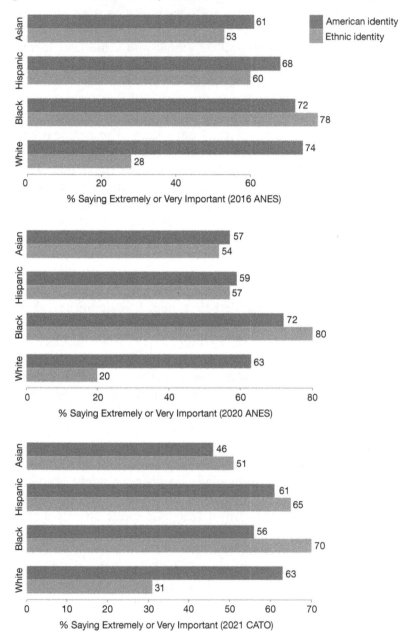

Assimilation Then and Now

Hispanics, and 0.32 for Asians. In other words, those who express a stronger sense of ethnic identity also identify *more* strongly with America, not less. Moreover, in the 2016 ANES, which included questions about love of country and feelings about the American flag, a strong sense of ethnic identification is positively, albeit weakly, related to patriotic sentiment in all ethnic groups. Predictably, a strong sense of American identity and patriotism are much more strongly related, affirming that seeing oneself as an American fosters national loyalty among immigrants.

Looking now at the generational differences reported in Figure 4.2, support for the assimilation trajectory does emerge, at least for Hispanics, the very group Huntington found most worrying. In the Cato survey, ethnic identification falls from 70% among the foreign-born to 62% in the third generation, the native-born with native-born parents; a strong American identification rises from 57% to 69%. The 2020 ANES results are similar: a strong ethnic identification falls from 68% among the foreign-born to 47% in the third generation; the strength of one's American identity rises from 57% to 64%. Among Asian respondents, neither the Cato survey nor ANES finds this pattern of change. However, other studies find that the length of time one has lived in the United States, a kind of proxy for generation, predicts whether Asian-Americans identify themselves just as American.[19] One might speculate also that the growing intermarriage of Asians and whites in the third generation, and the tendency for their offspring to identify as white, will boost the tendency of people with Asian ancestry to have strong American identities.

If ethnic and national identities are complementary and one sees oneself as a "hyphenated" American, what happens when push comes to shove? In other words, which of one's dual attachments is considered more important and how does this choice affect other attitudes? We measure identity choice with a simple procedure. The questions about the importance of one's ethnic and American identities provided five response options ranging from "not at all," coded 1, to "extremely," coded 5. To create a scale ranging from 0 to 1 these answers were rescored as 0, 0.25, 0.50, 0.75 and 1. Then the ethnic identification score was subtracted

Immigration in the Court of Public Opinion

Figure 4.2. Immigrant Generational Differences in Ethnic and American Identification

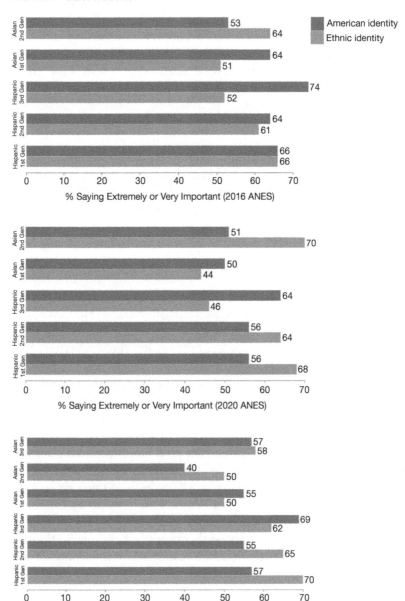

Assimilation Then and Now

from the American identification score to create three groups: American Identity More Important, Identities Equally Important, and Ethnicity More Important.

Figure 4.3 shows how respondents in the 2016 and 2020 ANES made these choices.[20] Again there is a sharp difference between whites and the three minority groups. For whites, American identity has priority by a wide margin – 67% to 3% in both 2016 and 2020. For blacks the dominant choice is to give equal importance to their ethnic and American identities, but "Race First" is a more common choice than "America First." Hispanics and Asians also make equal importance the most common choice, but here relatively more respondents prioritized their American than their ethnic identity, although the differences are small.

Generational change shows the increasing prioritization of American identity. In the 2016 ANES, the proportion of Hispanics giving more importance to their national identity rose from 25% among the foreign-born to 43% in the third generation; in the 2020 ANES the equivalent figures are 17% and 42%, the latter a slightly higher proportion than those who opted for equal importance. The ANES surveys did not include more than a handful of third-generation Asian immigrants, so to test the assimilation model for this group we turn to the National Asian American and Pacific Islander Survey of 2016. The results from that study parallel what we have reported above. Strong ethnic identification persists across the three immigrant generations and there is no great rise in the importance of American identity. But when one looks at prioritization, the tendency to give more importance to one's American than ethnic identity increases substantially as one moves from the foreign-born Asian respondents to those in the third generation.[21]

Age, higher education, a Republican partisan identification and conservative self-designation are associated with prioritizing one's American identity. Among Hispanic respondents, speaking English rather than Spanish at home also increases the tendency to give greater importance to one's American identity.

Prioritizing one's American identity is associated with stronger feelings of patriotism and with support for cultural assimilation.

Immigration in the Court of Public Opinion

Figure 4.3. The Prioritization of Identities

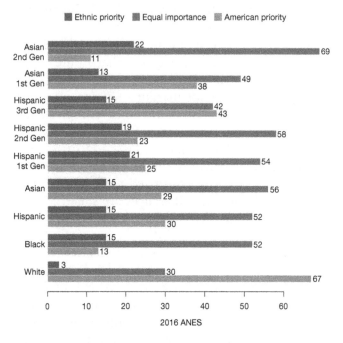
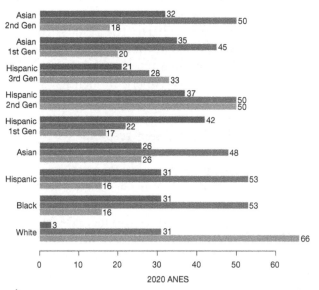

Assimilation Then and Now

The 2020 ANES asked respondents whether they agreed that "minorities should adapt to American customs." In every ethnic group by a large margin, those who give greater importance to their American rather than their ethnic identity more strongly favored cultural assimilation. The same pattern appears in more muted form when the survey asked whether speaking English and following American customs are important for making one a "true American." An important finding is that the attitudes of people who gave equal importance to their ethnic and American identities consistently were closer to those who prioritized American identity rather than ethnicity. A dual or hyphenated identity among minorities is compatible with an acceptance of cultural assimilation, *pace* Teddy Roosevelt.

Identity choice also is linked to opinions about immigration policy. In the 2020 ANES, there are generational differences in beliefs about whether immigration should be increased or decreased, with the third generation slightly more in favor of a reduced level than the foreign-born. A similar gap appears when people are asked if they favor building a wall on the Southern border. But these differences in opinion are enlarged when one considers the prioritization of one's American rather than one's ethnic identity. Among Asian respondents who prioritized American identity, 35% said the level of legal immigration should be increased, compared to 63% among those who said their ethnic identity was more important to them. Among Hispanic respondents, the comparable figures are 30% and 52%. Among Asians putting their American identity first, 40% favored building the wall, compared to only 6% among those whose ethnic identity was given priority. Among the Hispanic respondents, the equivalent figures were 33% and 5%. Among the two ethnic groups populated largely by recent immigrants, a strong American identity is associated with immigration attitudes that are far closer to those of whites than to their co-ethnics who order their dual identities differently. One dimension of assimilation, the development of a strong national identity, spills over onto another – preferences on immigration policy, a topic at the heart of the debate over the absorption of newcomers.

Immigration in the Court of Public Opinion

Hispanics and Asians are gradually transitioning, across generations, to prioritizing their American identity. In the Cato survey of 2021, just as in the earlier Los Angeles studies summarized in Jack Citrin and David Sears' *American Identity and the Politics of Multiculturalism* (2014), the noncitizen immigrants were the most likely to give greater importance to their ethnic identity; naturalized immigrants and native-born Hispanics and Asians were more likely to identify strongly as Americans. Ethnic identification was durable even in later generations of Hispanics and Asians, but each successive generation was more likely to give more importance to their American identity and to fuse this choice with greater patriotism, another indication of assimilation.

It is too early to tell for certain whether ethnic identification among Hispanics and Asians will fade as it did among the European immigrants of the late nineteenth and early twentieth centuries. As Roberto Suro has argued, much about the integration and acceptance of immigrants and their descendants hinges on the choices of these groups' visible advocates as well as those of the broader society.[22] The continuing influx of immigrants from Latin America and Asia, as well as a political climate that values group consciousness and its employment in the pursuit of tangible and symbolic benefits, may slow this process. Still far and away the dominant evidence of several decades of public opinion supports the assimilation narrative of the gradual "Americanization" of immigrants, now as in the past.

This includes the gradual shedding, or attrition, of ethnic "labels" altogether. According to economists Brian Duncan and Stephen Trejo, approximately 30% of third-generation Mexican Americans (those with Mexican immigrant grandparents) no longer identify as Hispanic.[23] The Pew Research Center put the figure at slightly under one in four but using a methodology likely to miss many individuals with Latin American ancestry.[24] By the fourth generation, ethnic identification may drop to half or less of descendants of Mexican immigrants. Rates of ethnic attrition among descendants of Asian immigrants appear to be comparable. Those who drop the ethnic label altogether tend to be among the most culturally, socially, and economically assimilated.

Assimilation Then and Now

Since almost all popular discourse about, and most academic study of, assimilation examines only the subset of descendants of immigrants who continue to self-label in ethnic terms (often this is used as a screen for surveys), virtually all of it substantially understates the true pace and scope of assimilation in contemporary American life.

The transition from a foreign to an American identity is pushed along by structural factors such as upward mobility, residential integration, personal interactions with members of the mainstream, and intermarriage. As American parents have known for generations, resistance to the forces of assimilation is usually futile. Those who long for their children to keep up ancestral customs and language, and fear that a son or daughter will "marry out," are likely to have to accommodate themselves to the realities of the melting pot. Groups, such as the ultra-orthodox Satmar Jews in Brooklyn, that do manage to stave off assimilation do so only through extreme isolation in a hierarchical and closed community – and as recent popular depictions of those who leave its confines have illustrated, even they struggle against the lure of the broader society.

Which Version of Assimilation Do Americans Support?

The criteria for belonging to America have been debated from the country's beginning, with exclusive standards such as native birth, race, and religion pitted against inclusive norms such as individualism, loyalty, and commitment to democratic values. A large literature assesses public conceptions of national identity by asking which of a range of attributes, including both "ethnic" and "civic" contenders, are important for making someone a "true" American.[25] Although a residue of nativist sentiment emphasizing the "ethnic" criteria of native birth, race, and religion appears in these surveys, they all find higher levels of support for "civic" principles such as "treating people of all backgrounds equally" and "respecting our laws and institutions." Predictably, those

Immigration in the Court of Public Opinion

with ethnic conceptions of American identity are more opposed to increasing immigration and more insistent that minorities should blend into the cultural mainstream.[26]

While immigration of people different from "us" has always sparked concern about risks to national identity, events can alter beliefs about the normative foundations of national identity. For example, Pew Research Center surveys found that American views about national identity were more restrictive in 2016, when immigration was a salient issue in the presidential campaign, than in 2020.[27] The proportion saying it was very or somewhat important to be born in the country to be a true American dropped from 55% to 35%; the importance of being a Christian dropped from 51% to 35%, and even the widely accepted belief that speaking English is a criterion for being an American fell from 92% to 77%. Speaking English, however, was always more important than place of birth in defining national identity.

The 2020 ANES survey asked about the importance of being born in America, speaking English, and following American customs for being a "true" American. Figure 4.4 compares the answers of the four main ethnic groups and immigrant generations, summing the proportions saying these criteria were either "very" or "fairly" important. The idea that being native-born is important for making one truly American received substantial support, ranging from 64% among blacks, almost all of whom were native-born, to 30% among Asians, where a large proportion were foreign-born. Interestingly, this belief was about equally prevalent among whites (46%) and Hispanics (48%). Native-born Hispanics and Asians were more likely than their foreign-born co-ethnics to say that this was important in making one truly American, suggesting perhaps that this response is partly a statement about one's own feeling of legitimate membership.

Speaking English is considered an important marker of American identity by all four ethnic groups, although this belief is somewhat more widespread among whites and blacks. Among Hispanics and Asians, even a large majority of the foreign-born, whose primary language often remains their original tongue, endorse the importance of speaking English – certainly a pragmatic recognition of

Assimilation Then and Now

Figure 4.4. What Makes Someone a "True" American?

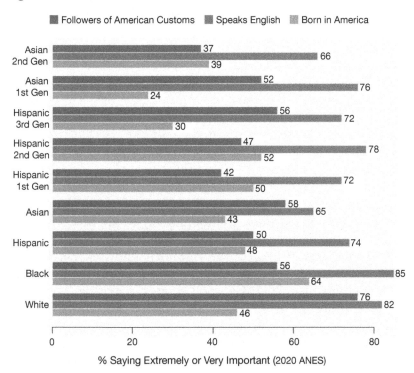

% Saying Extremely or Very Important (2020 ANES)

the role linguistic assimilation would play in economic progress and social acceptance.

Language is the basis of communication and a visible marker of a group's identity. Although the United States is ethnically one of the most heterogeneous nations in the world, linguistically it is quite homogeneous. Nevertheless, the influx of immigrants from non-English-speaking regions after 1965 sparked conflicts over language policy. Demands for language rights by advocates of multiculturalism provoked opponents to argue that demands for bilingualism threatened national unity. Referendums and legislation in over twenty states beginning in the mid-1980s declared English the official language there. Polls have consistently shown that most of the public support a law that would make English the official national language. In a 2000 General Social Survey

(GSS), 79% of white and 75% of black respondents favored this. Other surveys find small majorities of US-born Hispanics agreeing.[28]

Huntington and others have feared the development of Spanish-speaking enclaves and raised the prospect of an American version of Quebec emerging in the Southwest. But there is no evidence that Hispanic immigrants are hostile to learning English. The reality is that English is the dominant language by the second generation and beyond. Confirming the finding of the 2015 Pew survey cited above, the 2020 ANES found that fully 84% of the third-generation Hispanic respondents said they spoke only English at home compared to just 3% who primarily spoke Spanish. English-dominant Hispanics were more likely to identify as Americans, more likely to be patriotic, and more likely to say that minorities should blend into the mainstream.

These declarations reflect the view that knowing English is a prerequisite for the upward mobility and political incorporation of immigrants. The 2000 GSS poll showed majorities approving bilingual education programs that speed the learning of English, accepting the use of bilingual ballots, and believing that it would be good if more Americans learned a foreign language. In the Cato survey, only a minority of 35% said they were bothered to hear a language other than English spoken in public. Opposition to bilingualism predictably is associated with a desire to limit immigration, but for most of the public "English Only" seems to have given way to "English First." The reality of linguistic assimilation on the ground should diminish fears of cultural balkanization.

A recent study by Nick McRee and Mark Setzler gives additional support for the staying power of assimilationist forces.[29] They used data from a nationally representative longitudinal survey of adolescents to examine individual-level determinants of non-electoral participation, voter registration, voting, economic individualism, governmental trust, and partisanship. The results compared young Latino immigrants to their white, black, and non-immigrant Hispanic peers. The authors conclude that, "in contrast to the assumptions of segmented assimilation theory and

Assimilation Then and Now

nativist political rhetoric, we find no evidence supporting the idea that young Hispanics are resistant to any aspect of political assimilation. To the contrary, the patterns of political engagement and support for core American political values among first-generation and second-generation Hispanic youth closely mirror those of other young Americans."

Assimilation versus Multiculturalism

The belief that minorities should adopt some American customs and that doing so is important for making one a true American expresses the assimilationist ethos. However, as noted above, most people voicing support for cultural assimilation are not insisting that immigrants shed their original traditions. Multiculturalism rejects the pressure to acculturate, emphasizing instead the virtues of preserving one's original customs and claiming that governments should assure this outcome. According to the Canadian scholars Keith Banting and Will Kymlicka,[30] multiculturalist policies include official recognition of multiculturalism as a defining feature of a country's identity, and government assistance for ethnic organizations, bilingual education, media programs with multicultural content, dual citizenship, and affirmative action programs that guarantee minority groups greater representation in political and social institutions.

Broadly speaking, multicultural policies that allocate rights and government funds based on group identities are unpopular. As Jack Citrin and his colleagues showed twenty years ago, strong majorities of Americans from all ethnic backgrounds reject affirmative action (except, in some cases, when it benefits their own group) in education and employment, and certainly any notion of quotas awarded to groups with respect to representation in government.[31] Although majorities are supportive of "transitional" bilingual education to give recently arrived immigrant students the opportunity to keep up with their studies while learning English, large bipartisan and cross-ethnic majorities reject "cultural maintenance-style" bilingual education that would

Immigration in the Court of Public Opinion

permit public-school students to continue taking many classes in their own native languages through high school. More recent studies confirm that opposition to such hard forms of multiculturalism remains strong.

A convenient summary measure of this opposition to hard multiculturalism comes from a question on the 2014 national identity module of the General Social Survey (part of the International Social Survey Program, to which we will return in chapter 5). It asked whether the government should help minorities preserve their traditions. Only 17% of respondents agreed that it should. A mere 1% agreed strongly, suggesting the existence of almost no committed multiculturalist constituency in the mass public. Sixty percent of the public disagreed with this idea, which is the centerpiece of multiculturalist ideology as a political program.

If Americans reject hard multiculturalism, what do they want? We begin by focusing on the general question of whether people prefer minorities "to blend into the larger society as in the ideal of the melting pot" or "maintain their distinct cultures and traditions." This question has been asked many times by GSS and ANES since 1992. Blending in is always the majority position with an average margin of about 60% to 40%, with whites and blacks more disapproving than Hispanics or Asians of the multiculturalist position of preserving immigrants' original cultures.[32]

The 2021 Cato survey provides a more recent look at this question. More respondents agree (43%) than disagree (23%) that "when the country's ethnic makeup changes, the idea of its identity also changes." Yet 59% believe that "the United States is a country with an essential American culture and values that immigrants take on when they arrive." On the standard "blend into the mainstream versus maintain one's distinct cultures" question, 73% of whites, 63% of blacks, and fully 67% of both Hispanics and Asians chose the assimilationist position of immigrants changing to blend into the larger society.

A series of responses indicates mixed views about the progress of assimilation. When asked if "immigrants today come from cultures very different than previous and so have more trouble assimilating to the American way of life," 39% agreed and 29% disagreed,

Assimilation Then and Now

with the rest taking no position. Interestingly, there were no differences among ethnic groups or immigrant generations. When asked if immigrants who had arrived in the past twenty years had in fact adopted essential values rather than retaining their own cultures, answers in the sample were evenly divided. However, the survey found that Asians (64%) and Hispanics (58%) were more likely than whites (48%) and blacks (47%) to say that recent immigrants to the United States were assimilating, a position which is closer to the facts on the ground.

As the overwhelmingly positive responses to questions about immigrants' economic and cultural impacts reviewed in chapter 2 indicate, these responses do not signal alarm about a gradual pace of assimilation. One important reason is that Americans are not, by and large, threatened by immigrants' retention of a great many aspects of their ancestral heritages.

In this view, the blend/maintain survey item poses a false dichotomy. For a large majority of the public, the preferred answer is "some of both." When asked in the 2013 GSS national identity module whether immigrants should retain their own cultures, give them up, or both retain their cultures and adopt the host country's too, 86% chose the middle option – a ringing endorsement of the modern, pluralistic understanding of liberal assimilation. Only 3% wanted immigrants to simply maintain their own cultures and 5% to give them up. Evidently, the public sees no insurmountable tension between being ethnic and being American.

The Cato survey included an innovative question that probed beyond expressions of support for adopting American customs in the abstract. Respondents were asked how important it was for immigrants to display specific traits or behaviors ranging from being loyal to the United States to celebrating American holidays to adopting American styles of dress.

Table 4.1 presents the full set of answers for the sample as a whole and for each ethnic group. The results again clearly show that Americans endorse a "thin" form of assimilation that stresses universalistic attributes such as loyalty to the United States, self-reliance, and speaking English fluently. Even among the native whites, whom assimilation theorists deem the carrier

Immigration in the Court of Public Opinion

of mainstream norms, only 28% say that immigrants should celebrate American holidays, 20% say immigrants should love George Washington and Abraham Lincoln, 14% say they should adopt Christian beliefs, and only 13% call for them to wear American styles of dress. Although the levels of agreement vary from group to group, the rank order of what should be expected of immigrants is the same across ethnic groups and immigrant generations. This consensus leaves a lot of room for immigrants to follow their own customs within a general acceptance of the inclusive values of patriotism, individualism, and learning English. Public expectations of immigrants, then, do not resemble the old-fashioned nativist program of cleansing immigrants of their past traditions.

Table 4.1. How Important Is It to You That Immigrants...?

% Saying Extremely or Very Important	Total	White	Black	Hispanic	Asian
Be loyal to the United States	71	76	56	63	53
Be self-reliant	69	73	59	57	53
Speak English fluently	53	55	47	49	35
Become friends with American-born members of the community	40	43	33	35	33
Adopt American habits and customs	37	38	32	33	27
Adopt American history as part of their own	34	35	32	33	27
Celebrate American holidays	28	28	21	32	21
Love George Washington and Abraham Lincoln	20	20	14	25	17
Adopt Christian religious belief	16	14	22	25	13
Adopt American style of dress	14	13	15	19	14
Be of European descent	7	6	9	13	8

Source: Cato survey 2021

Assimilation Then and Now

Most Americans continue to believe that there is a common culture, that immigrants should adopt it, and that over time most will. But the set of beliefs and customs that immigrants are expected to adopt is narrow, and there is no accompanying dictate that immigrants rush to surrender their own heritage – though, over time, the empirical evidence indicates that the great majority will. Here the public is at odds with government, academic, business, and media elites whose mantra of Diversity, Equity, and Inclusion embodies the multiculturalist ethos of accommodating minority cultural norms. Indeed, the Biden administration has banned the use of the term assimilation in official statements, opting for integration as the more politically correct alternative.[33]

Another Look at Assimilation to What?

The idea of assimilation assumes that there is consensus on the existence of dominant norms which over time come to govern the attitudes and behavior of immigrants. These norms may evolve, but for assimilation to be studied there must be something there, a core set of values that are the end point of the process of integrating newcomers. But what if there is no One America, but congeries of warring tribes, each with its own regional base, distinct ideology, social following, and, most importantly, its own version of American history and what it means to be an American? A growing literature portrays the United States as hopelessly fragmented, a country whose common identity is at best frayed and at worst in shreds. What then is an immigrant from Mars, anxious to fit in and become a full-fledged member of the political community, to do? Whose standards are the end point of the assimilation trajectory? It would not be surprising if our Martian were dazed and confused, perhaps opting in the end for the dominant culture of where in the country his spaceship landed.

Hispanic and Asian immigrants are assimilating by the criteria of identifying as Americans, learning English, and being patriotic. And their work ethic and effort to get ahead are well documented

Immigration in the Court of Public Opinion

and recognized by most. The main nativist fears harbored by a small minority of the public are misguided. Indeed, those worrying about the future of American identity should look elsewhere. Beliefs about the worth of assimilation now are polarized on partisan and ideological lines. Evidence reviewed by Zach Goldberg in *Tablet* suggests that young, educated white liberal Democrats are less attached to their American identity.[34] They are more likely to deny that there is anything distinctive about American values and identity and less likely than other Americans to say they love their country. The Cato survey found that 38% of Democrats compared to 13% of Republicans said they thought of themselves more as global citizens than as Americans; 58% of self-identified strong liberals compared to 16% of strong conservatives defined themselves as globalists. Democrats (49%) and strong liberals (33%) were far less likely to say that their American identity was very important to them than Republicans (77%) or strong conservatives (86%). Similar gaps appeared when people were asked whether it is important for immigrants to be loyal, self-reliant, and fluent in English. The nation is divided not just about immigration policy but about what it means to be an American, with those holding the Woke ethos espousing the image of the country as irredeemably racist confronting believers in the old Whig notion of an exceptional nation with a history of progress toward equality. If there is segmented assimilation, its foundations may lie in the fragmentation of American politics rather than changes in the structure of the US economy or differences between today's immigrants and those of yesteryear. Still, for the moment, wokeness is a surprisingly white phenomenon. Ironically, a major obstacle to its acceptance in the Democratic Party has been that minority voters, especially immigrants and their offspring, by and large simply don't buy it.

5

American Exceptionalism?

"American Exceptionalism" is the idea that there is something unique about the American way of life, that this is a country free of the hierarchies and restraints bedeviling old Europe. This self-image is pervasive from the arrival of the first colonist-laden ships bound for Jamestown and Plymouth in the early seventeenth century. Since then, travelers, thinkers, pundits, and dreamers have all pondered what makes America *America*, and what makes Americans *American*. Why are Americans so obsessed with rugged individualism – liberty and freedom from government's interference with their rights? (Just contrast the Declaration of Independence's pursuit of "life, liberty and happiness" with the very different emphasis on "peace, order, and good government" emphasized in the founding charter of America's neighbor to the north.) Why are they so actively religious, and why does this so often express itself through the so-called "Prosperity Gospel"? Why – a question asked repeatedly since the late nineteenth century – is there no socialism in the United States? Why are Americans so eager to sue, so outspoken about the right to own firearms, so stubbornly opposed to adopting the metric system?

When it comes to immigration, matters are no different. There is a huge iconography about America as a "nation of immigrants" distinct from others in rooting the boundaries of the national community in political culture rather than ancestry. In historian Richard Hofstadter's phrase, "it has been our fate as a nation not to have ideologies, but to be one."[1] The poet Crevecoeur, in *Letters*

Immigration in the Court of Public Opinion

From an American Farmer (1782), went so far as to suggest that America was breeding a new kind of man, one who, "leaving behind him all his ancient prejudices and manners, receives new ones from the new mode of life he has embraced, the government he obeys, and the new rank he holds. He is neither a European nor the descendant of a European; hence that strange mixture of blood, which you will find in no other country."

To the many contemporary observers who see the immigration politics of today as another round in a long history of exclusion and nativism, this inclusive portrait of a diverse country with a civic identity is inaccurate if not hopelessly naïve. In their critical view, the US is no more open than other nations. Or its welcome is conditional on the financial interests of a capitalist class in exploiting a pliable foreign labor force. If the country is distinctive at all, it is in its individualist sink-or-swim mindset, which fosters callousness toward the struggles of the poor, and in its history of racial oppression, which lays the groundwork for incorporating non-white immigrants as marginalized "others."

Without necessarily endorsing this dark image of American immigration, much cross-national research assumes that similar forces shape immigration attitudes in the US and other countries. Labor economists studying the role of job threat, for example, have applied their theories to workers across developed countries. Group-centered psychological theories, too, have imported presumably universal theories of group relations to broad sets of host nations, though of course the specific hypotheses are tailored to the context in question – which groups are dominant, how racial categories are defined and understood, and so on.[2] Much of this cross-national research does not even consider the question of whether America is different. And what research has taken up the question of exceptionalism explicitly casts doubt on the thesis.[3]

Is there, then, a case for American exceptionalism when it comes to immigration? Does America's history of immigration make its citizens more willing to accept immigrants than people elsewhere? Are they more sanguine about its consequences? Are they more willing to tolerate an ecumenical, culturally pluralistic vision of national identity? In this chapter, we use survey evidence from several countries to find out if American attitudes toward immigration are noticeably different.

The Evidence

Any test for "exceptionalism" must be comparative. But whom should we compare Americans *to*, and on what basis? Our focus on public opinion takes us to cross-national surveys that have attempted to standardize their content across many languages and cultures and to track responses over several decades. The best studies recruit their respondents similarly across countries and ask relatively abstract questions that do not depend on rich contextual knowledge.

An ideal candidate for our inquiry here is the International Social Survey Program (ISSP), an academic consortium that has for many years designed standardized content for surveys conducted in numerous countries. Here we analyze the "National Identity" module (mentioned in chapter 4) which has a set of questions about immigration, diversity, and nationalism. This module was initially fielded in 1995, repeated in 2003, and then again in 2013. The content has evolved somewhat over the years, but the core of the module has remained intact throughout this period, and we limit ourselves to these recurrent questions.

The question of exceptional relative to *whom* doesn't have one obvious answer. If a big part of America's self-image is as a nation of immigrants, then a logical comparison is to the "Old World" from where those immigrants originally came. Here we stand on the shoulders of giants: Alexis de Tocqueville, who contrasted America to France in his monumental *Democracy in America*; Karl Marx, who developed his thinking about social class struggle to a large degree through the lens of America's struggle to abolish slavery; and a long line of amateur and professional social scientists who followed in their wake.[4] From this it follows that we should compare Americans' attitudes to those of the citizens of Western and Northern Europe whose nations historically are known more for sending than receiving

Immigration in the Court of Public Opinion

immigrants, have much stronger ethno-cultural heritages, and have only recently had to deal with the kind of large, diverse immigrant influxes that have been central to American history from its beginning. While not every Western European country is surveyed in every ISSP year, we have data from Austria, Belgium, France, Germany, the UK, Ireland, the Netherlands, Portugal, and Spain. Northern Europe, which we keep distinct from Western Europe in this analysis, is represented by Denmark, Finland, Sweden, and Norway.

But something to keep in mind is that America is not the only "nation of immigrants" around. At least three other developed immigrant-receiving democracies fit that bill: Canada, Australia, and New Zealand. All these "settler states" share a trajectory of being explored by Europeans in the seventeenth century and colonized by them (mostly the British) in the eighteenth and early nineteenth centuries. All have experienced and absorbed both multiple waves of immigrants over their various histories as well as major contractions, often in near-parallel with their American cousins.

The United States experienced a major influx of immigrants in the late 1800s, and by 1910 the foreign-born comprised roughly 15% of the population, a proportion only recently matched in the wake of the liberalizing reforms we discussed in chapter 1. Along similar lines, Canada's foreign-born share of its total population eclipsed 20% by the early twentieth century, followed by a similar (albeit less dramatic) ebb thereafter. Canada, Australia, New Zealand, and the US all sharply restricted immigration from Asia in the late nineteenth century, and all adopted (at various points) ostensibly race-neutral policies – think poll taxes and literacy tests – intended to close the door to less "desirable" immigrants. The details of their policies vary, but after World War II all four of these countries undertook a liberalization of immigration rules resulting in ethnic diversification. Fortunately, the ISSP national identity modules included Australia, Canada, and New Zealand in 1995 and 2003, allowing comparison with the US over a somewhat truncated time span. In short, we examine the possibility that the Anglo-American "settler states" are all exceptional

102

American Exceptionalism?

relative to the Old World, and that the US stands out in certain ways even within this group.

An important caveat when assessing the evidence is that many survey questions allude explicitly or implicitly to context. For example, saying one wants more immigration in a country that accepts very few immigrants or selects heavily on professional skill to import other countries' elite and upwardly mobile is very different from saying one wants more in a country that accepts many and opens its doors to the world's huddled masses. Here we have focused only on countries that accept large numbers of immigrants. The US has a higher foreign-born percentage than most of the European nations in our sample but a somewhat lower percentage than Canada and Australia. But the US stands out among all the countries in our sample for the very limited role that education and job skills play in selecting legal immigrants. The US also stands out for its relatively high volume of illegal immigration. Demands for heightened border security mean different things in a setting where illegal entry is rampant than in one in which illegal immigration is less common and more driven by visa over-stayers (who entered legally and were vetted). Significantly, too, the origins of immigration flows differ a great deal. Europe has received much more immigration from the Middle East and North Africa, and antipathy toward immigrants from this region, especially Muslims, appears to be especially pronounced. All of this is to say that comparisons need to be treated with caution, taking stock not only of average differences in responses to poll questions but the contexts that those questions reference.

Controlling Borders and Inflows

One fundamental aspect of immigration policy is border control. As explored in chapters 2 and 3, this concerns how many people are allowed to immigrate legally and whether this number should be increased or decreased, and the related (yet distinct) consideration is how effectively the government excludes those immigrants who come without permission. The ISSP survey asked in all three

Immigration in the Court of Public Opinion

iterations of the national identity module both the (by now) familiar "levels" item (scored here from 0 = "restrictions should be increased a lot" to 4 = "restrictions should be decreased a lot") and another question phrased "(R's country) should take stronger measures to exclude illegal immigrants," coded here from 0 = "strongly disagree" to 4 = "strongly agree." The average score for the US and each comparison group is displayed in Figure 5.1. Two further points before proceeding. First, notice that around each mean score we have our usual estimate of statistical error, and a lack of vertical overlap comparing estimates indicates that the difference is likely real and not an artifact of the sampling process. Second, patches of incomplete coverage exist because not every country group was surveyed in all three waves, and because occasionally specific questions were omitted in certain countries.

In general, people lean to the restrictive side on these measures, assuming a "neutral" point of "2" on the scale. One interesting pattern is liberalization over time in three of the four sets of countries. But Western Europe's turn toward greater restriction in

Figure 5.1. Inflows and Border Control

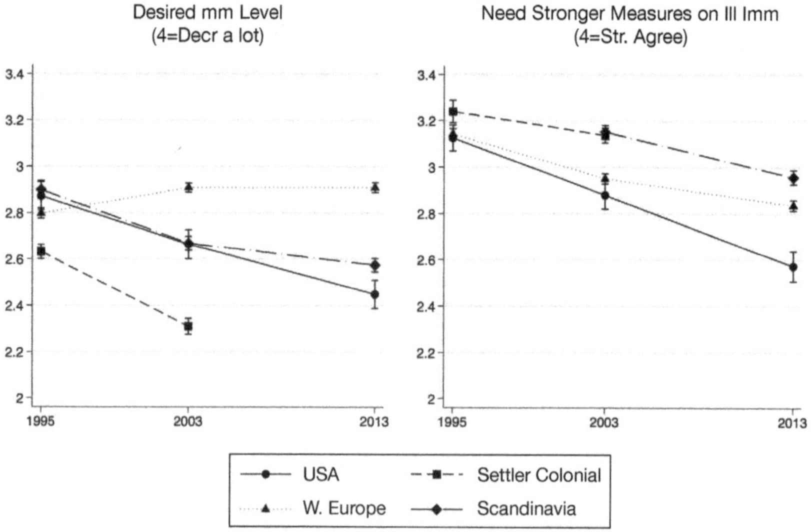

Source: ISSP 1995, 2003, 2013

American Exceptionalism?

numbers admitted from 1995 to 2003 (and continuing on roughly the same plane through 2013) contrasts sharply with the US trend. It is worth noting as well that, as we discussed in previous chapters, 1995 was the pinnacle of recorded American opposition to increasing immigration, and this has dissipated almost without interruption (the 9/11 attacks being the exception) ever since. In Europe, the flood of refugees from the Middle East began in the middle of the 2000s; opposition soon surfaced and now closing the borders to such migrants is pervasive. With respect to strengthening measures against illegal immigrants, all four sets of countries clustered together in supporting a tougher policy in 1995 (opinion hovers around three-quarters of the way toward the scale's maximum score), and all have generally softened their positions since.

Are there signs of a uniquely American outlook? The answer is an emphatic "yes" relative to the countries of Western Europe, "increasingly so" relative to Scandinavia, and a more qualified "somewhat" relative to the settler countries. Taking the "levels" item first, the "settler states" countries (Australia, Canada, and New Zealand) are altogether more sanguine about immigrant admissions than the US, which seems to cluster with Western Europe and Scandinavia in 1995, an admittedly unusual year in the US with respect to the salience of reducing immigration. The differences widen significantly over time, however. In the large immigrant-receiving democracies of Western Europe, the public, in fact, becomes more hostile over time. In other settings attitudes liberalize, but the trend in the US is stronger, opening a larger gap with Scandinavia. And we know that this trend has accelerated in the US since. Thus, on the question of the volume of legal admissions, the US has since the 1990s moved from similarity to the Old World to a position much closer to its settler nation brethren in distinctive openness to high levels of immigration.

Turning to support for stronger measures to curb illegal immigration, somewhat puzzlingly for a country where debates over illegal immigration take up so much political oxygen, Figure 5.1 provides clear evidence of exceptionalism on the "pro" side: Americans are without exception *less* supportive of strong border

Immigration in the Court of Public Opinion

enforcement measures than any of the other three comparison groups; the distinction is small in 1995, but by 2013 the US stood out as quite a bit more liberal than the others. This of course is before Trump made border control a salient issue and before the growing partisan polarization on most aspects of immigration policy. But as we saw in chapters 1 and 2, these developments seem to have pushed Americans at least temporarily in a more tolerant, *pro*-immigrant direction. If anything, these differences would have remained the same or widened in the intervening years, heightening American exceptionalism not only relative to Europe but also to the other settler nations.

Consequences of Immigration

Are "nations of immigration" generally persuaded that the consequences of immigration are benign if not altogether positive? Figure 5.2 maps out by country group and year people's level of agreement or disagreement with the following statements:

– "Immigrants increase crime rates," coded such that 0 = disagree strongly and 4 = agree strongly.
– "Immigrants are generally good for [R's country's] economy," coded such that 0 = agree strongly and 4 = disagree strongly.
– "Immigrants take jobs away from people who were born in [R's country]," coded such that 0 = disagree strongly and 4 = agree strongly.
– "Immigrants make [R's country] more open to new ideas and cultures," coded such that 0 = agree strongly and 4 = disagree strongly.

Figure 5.2 is set up so that all questions are coded with "anti-immigrant" responses higher on the vertical axis than "pro-immigrant" ones. Since each question has the same basic response categories, we can contrast sentiment easily across items. On average, people are ambivalent or at any rate not especially extreme: the mean response to most of these questions hovers around the scale midpoint of "2," which captures a neutral

American Exceptionalism?

Figure 5.2. Consequences of Immigration

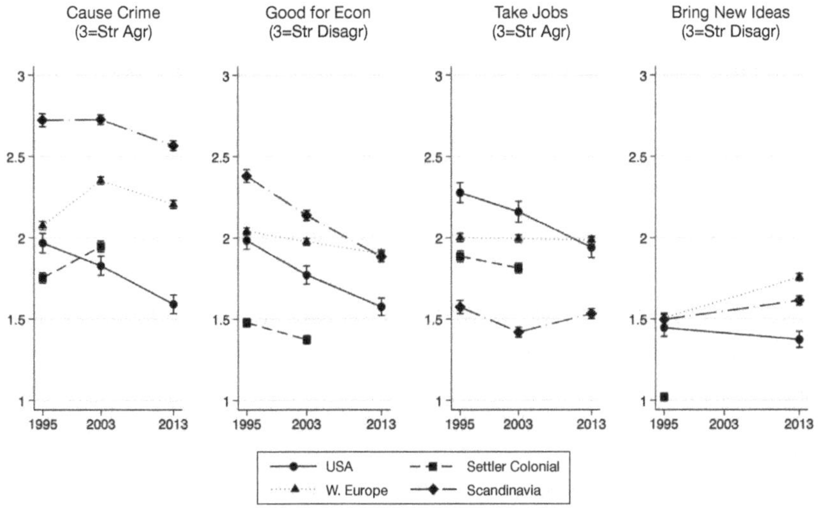

Source: ISSP 1995, 2003, 2013

stance. On three of the four measures (the exception is the item about "new ideas and cultures") the prevailing attitude has shifted to the positive over the period between 1995 and 2013. This is especially so for the items tied to jobs and the economy, less so for crime.

There is less in the way of an obvious pattern of differences among country groups, nor is there much consistency across items. Americans score among the most convinced that immigrants might "take jobs," although by 2013 they had become effectively neutral on this point, and no more negative than Western Europeans. On the other hand, they are consistently *less* likely than either Western European or Scandinavian respondents to tie immigration to crime. This is striking given all the rhetoric linking immigration (illegal immigration in particular) to public safety. One might wonder if these attitudes carried over to the Trump era. As we saw in chapter 2, using ANES data from 2020, they do. Only 26% of the sample agreed even somewhat that immigration, overall, increases crime rates, and only 4% felt this strongly (the distribution isn't quite

Immigration in the Court of Public Opinion

comparable to the ISSP because it used a five-point scale). Trump's argument associating illegal immigration with crime clearly has deep resonance in some corners of the American public, but it played to a relatively narrow audience that did not expand appreciably during his presidency.

America and the other settler nations are distinctively positive in believing that immigration does *not* have a corrosive effect on "ideas and culture" and in their attitudes about its impact on the economy. Here it must be said that the most recent comparison of the US to the settler states is from 2003, nearly twenty years ago and (it so happens) during the second most anti-immigrant period in recent US history, shortly after the 9/11 attacks. As of 2013, the US had continued to move toward a much more positive appraisal of these impacts, and given the findings reported in chapter 2 there is every reason to suppose that this trend has gained steam since.

The "ideas" question is admittedly somewhat ambiguous because the introduction of "new ideas" could in theory be good or bad. After all, the nativists of yore certainly believed that immigrants would bring new ideas to the US in the form of Popery or radicalism. But a separate item included in only the 2013 module leaves no doubt that Americans see less cultural threat from immigration than do most other nations. Asked whether immigrants undermine the nation's culture, only 3% of the US public strongly agreed, and 15% somewhat agreed. This is a lower level of strong and overall agreement than any European country in the sample except Iceland, where immigrants are a small number (recall that the other settler nations were not included in the 2013 wave). The figure of 59% of Americans who disagreed was also second highest to Iceland. The only countries that even came close were Spain, Switzerland, and Ireland, all of which recruit immigrants mostly from the EU or, in the case of Spain, also from Latin American countries which share its dominant language.

Overall, the data unambiguously show that there are distinctively more sanguine attitudes about the consequences of immigration among the settler nations, including the US. The unifying element is that all now regard themselves as a "nation of immigrants"; America is not exceptional in that way. Citizens of countries with

American Exceptionalism?

an origin story tied to immigration or a long history of absorbing successive waves of newcomers are much more positive about the influence of immigration on their society than those of old Europe, the original foil in the exceptionalism narrative. The positivity Americans in particular express is especially striking given the large presence of illegal immigrants and the strong balance toward admissions based on family ties rather than skills – characteristics that distinguish the US from the other three settler nations. In a country that takes fewer measures to control its immigration flow and tailor it to economic need, Americans are nonetheless distinctively optimistic that immigrants do not boost crime rates and that they help the economy.

Cultural Pluralism

Beyond simply gauging whether people want more or fewer immigrants and whether they think immigration is on balance a good thing, America might also be exceptional in how it evaluates ethnic diversity and cultural pluralism. Despite periodic outbursts of nativism, America's national identity has weathered the absorption of successive waves of immigrants that reshaped the demographic status quo. So, is America unique in its outlook toward increased ethnic diversity, in comparison both to countries of old Europe and to the other "settler" nations?

On this issue the ISSP's national identity module does ask relevant questions. One item is: "it is impossible for people who do not share (R's country's) customs and traditions to become fully (e.g., British)," with responses scored from 0 = "strongly disagree" to 4 = "strongly agree." A second is another agree/disagree item: "ethnic minorities should be given government assistance to preserve their customs and traditions," this time coded 0 = "strongly agree" to 4 = "strongly disagree." Lastly, the ISSP asks its respondents the core question about multiculturalism considered in chapter 4: "Some people say that it is better for a country if different racial and ethnic groups maintain their distinct customs and traditions. Others say that it is better if these groups adapt and blend into the larger society. Which of these views comes closer to your own?" For this item, we scored the answers 0 = "maintain their distinct customs" and 1 = "adapt to the larger society." The results, broken out by country groups, are shown in Figure 5.3.

In general, people in most country groups favor assimilation over multiculturalism. Even in the most liberal country groups (the US and settler countries), support for the notion that one needs to share a country's "customs and traditions" to truly be a member of that country's national community hangs around the scale's neutral point (2 on a scale running from 0 to 4). Similarly, when it comes to support for government efforts targeted at helping ethnic minorities "preserve their cultures and traditions," all groups lean toward the negative pole. Finally, there is a fairly pronounced (and consistent) tendency to favor immigrants'

Figure 5.3. Hostility to Cultural Pluralism

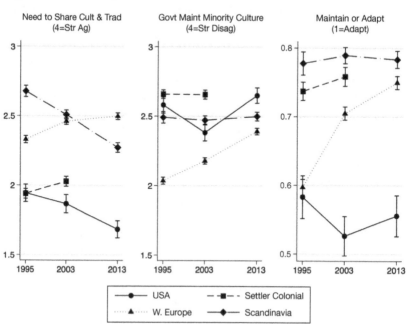

Source: ISSP 1995, 2003, 2013

American Exceptionalism?

"adapting" to the broader society rather than "maintaining distinct customs." People by and large favor maintaining established cultural norms and meanings of national identity and are wary of codifying cultural differences as part of a new idea of nationhood. Also of note is that unlike the responses presented in Figures 5.1 and 5.2, there seems to be less of an overall trend over time, perhaps indicating a higher degree of rigidity on these questions than on the more technocratic, policy-focused questions about immigration numbers, border integrity, and the societal consequences of immigration.

What is especially interesting, however, is that the US stands out from the pack on the two items tapping into abstract orientation to cultural pluralism: Americans are substantially more likely to *disagree* with the idea that one needs to share customs and traditions to be truly a part of the national community. Americans are also *far* more likely (about 20% on the response scale) to support minorities' maintaining their own culture and not having to adapt to the broader society, a difference that arguably reflects Americans' unwillingness to enforce culture conformity as part of a broader preference for personal liberty and individualism.

There is a certain irony here in that all the settler nations and most of the European countries we are looking at officially embraced multiculturalism as early as the 1970s and implemented measures such as group representation, media programs with multicultural content, and financial support for ethnic organizations. Notably too, these differences between the US and Europe on the need for cultural homogeneity pre-date much of the large-scale influx of Muslim immigration to Western Europe. This suggests that they are a function of enduring differences in political culture rather than just the characteristics of immigrant stocks and flows and the special challenges of bridging religious divides, although the relative paucity of Muslim immigrants in the United States arguably helps explain the relative absence of conflicts over the hijab, burqa, mosques, and minarets that have roiled Europe and French Canada. Recently the rhetorical pendulum in Europe has swung heavily toward assimilation. While earlier multiculturalist policies have not been dismantled, several countries are

Immigration in the Court of Public Opinion

introducing language and cultural knowledge as criteria for legal immigration. Given these developments and the rise of anti-immigrant parties throughout Europe, it is hard to imagine that more current data would narrow the observed gap with the United States.

The only area where the US finds itself close to the others is in opposition to government support for the maintenance of minority cultures. In fact, as of 2013, the US is if anything *more* antagonistic than the other nations to government efforts to preserve immigrants' distinct cultures. Is this a contradiction with Americans' pluralistic views on assimilation? On the contrary, it is the crucial other half of American exceptionalism. Here we see a laissez-faire attitude and a suspicion of government intervention in the private sphere, culture, or economy that is a hallmark of what Louis Hartz labeled the Liberal Tradition in America.

The contrast between abstract attitudes about diversity on the one hand and government support for helping preserve minority cultures on the other warrants further scrutiny because it bears directly on the question of how people think government and society ought to interact when it comes to ethnic pluralism. Put another way, it cuts to the heart of what it means for a country to be "multicultural." Figure 5.4 captures the individual-level *relationship* between these two attitudes, segregated by country group but not (for simplicity's sake) by year. In both cases, the "effect" is the item querying support for government assistance. In the left panel, the "cause" is support for the notion that one needs to share customs and traditions to be truly a part of the national community, and in the right panel, it is people's desire for minorities to "maintain" customs rather than adapt. Scoring is consistent with Figure 5.3 in all cases. Interpreting these data follows the procedure described above for Figures 3.1–3.3 in chapter 3: estimates above zero indicate a *positive* relationship (that scoring highly on one measure predicts scoring highly on the other), estimates below zero indicate a *negative* relationship (that scoring highly on one measure predicts scoring low on the other), and scores close to zero indicate that knowing what people say to one question tells us little or nothing about what they say on the

112

American Exceptionalism?

Figure 5.4. Predicting Government Support for Maintaining Minority Culture

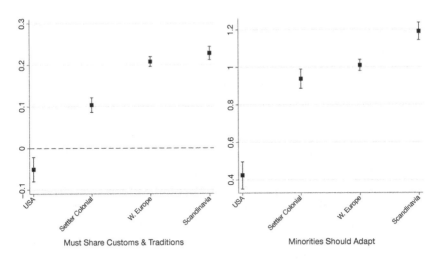

Source: ISSP 1995, 2003, 2013

other. As usual, we include confidence or uncertainty intervals for each estimate.

Here we find consistent evidence of a uniquely American outlook on cultural pluralism. In every other group of countries, people who want immigrants to maintain their distinct customs also tend to support government intervention to facilitate or bolster this aim. But for Americans, the connection is *much* weaker; it is there but much closer to zero with respect to the "maintain or adapt" item and, if anything, is stood on its head with respect to support for cultures and traditions. In both cases, the distinction with other immigrant-receiving countries is stark. This is not evidence in and of itself that Americans are more liberal or conservative on such issues than people elsewhere, but rather evidence that they are less likely to "connect" the two issues in their thinking. A distinctively larger share of Americans than in any other set of countries feels that immigrants should have the right to maintain their own customs, or even wants them to do so, but believes they should receive no help from the government in this endeavor.

Immigration in the Court of Public Opinion

Why? In our view, this stems less from anything peculiar about how Americans view diversity *per se*, and more to do with their general orientation about the role of government. In the other countries, people are more comfortable with a strong role for government in general, so to them it makes sense that if people value cultural pluralism in the abstract their government should be in the business of supporting it. In contrast, Americans tend to be warier of government interference in many aspects of their lives and so are less likely to support a strong government role in enforcing their abstract preferences on multiculturalism.

Taken together, the following are the attitudes that mark American exceptionalism when it comes to assimilation. First, there is a belief that immigrants should become self-sufficient and functional members of the host society, the minimalist version of assimilation we delineated in chapter 4. Second, beyond that, they have the right to choose whether to remain ethnic or blend in. What we have termed "thin assimilation," the dominant expectation of Americans, is quite compatible with what might be termed multiculturalism "lite," an acceptance of varied holidays, foods, music, and dress within the parameters of English-dominance and self-reliance. But third, immigrants should expect no help from the government or anyone else in preserving their customs. In America, preserving cultural pluralism is largely a voluntary affair, a matter of individual choice and initiative. No other country in the ISSP sample in any year evinces that pattern of beliefs.

Exceptionalism into the Trump Era

We have noted that an important limitation of the ISSP data is that it ends in 2013. Moreover, for the three non-US settler nations, the last available data is from twenty years ago, in 2003. In the intervening years, immigration has risen in political salience and become a more partisan and acrimonious issue at the elite level in many developed nations. Of course, in the US, it has become almost conventional to think about immigration politics as divided into the epochs Before Trump and After Trump.

American Exceptionalism?

Do the patterns we observed in the ISSP data continue to manifest themselves in more recent times? Has America in the Trump era become less "exceptional"? Although the different sets of survey items used precludes direct comparison to the ISSP data, all the available evidence suggests that the situation has changed little since 2013. Take, first, the Gallup World Survey.[5] Its Migrant Acceptance Index combines responses to three questions about immigration, all asked to publics from over two-thirds of all countries in the world: how they feel about immigrants living in their country, becoming their neighbors, and becoming part of their families. Higher scores mean people said these were viewed as good things rather than bad, and the highest possible score is 9.

In its 2016–17 survey, Gallup found that the two most accepting regions by far were Oceania (Australia and New Zealand) (8.0) and Northern America (7.9). The European Union scored far lower (5.9), lagging even slightly behind Sub-Saharan Africa and the Gulf Cooperation Council, and tying with Latin America and the Caribbean – itself a historically immigrant-receiving region, thus demonstrating that an immigrant history is insufficient to generate exceptionally pro-immigrant attitudes. In the 2019 survey, all four of the Anglo-American settler nations made the list of the top ten most accepting of immigrants, with Canada atop the list (8.5), closely followed by Australia and New Zealand (both 8.3), and trailed only slightly by the US (8.0). Only three European nations made the top ten, all of them very small: Iceland (8.4), Sweden (7.9), and Ireland (7.9). These questions only get at general positivity about migration and do not offer the granularity of the ISSP data even on expected consequences. But they leave no doubt at least that the settler nations, including the US, remain distinctive.

This of course does not mean that the US stands out as more pro-immigrant on all assessments and policy questions. As we saw earlier, Americans are more prone than others to worry that immigrants might take jobs from natives. Welfare also carries a particularly negative valence in American politics, and opposition to the idea that immigrants would use welfare was at the center

115

Immigration in the Court of Public Opinion

of the most effective anti-immigrant messaging in recent US political history, during the 1990s – a period when opposition to immigration briefly spiked on such concerns. So, unsurprisingly, on a question from the 2018 Pew Global Attitudes and Trends poll that asked whether immigrants are a benefit to the country because of their hard work and talents or a burden because they take jobs and use welfare, Americans do not stand out. They are slightly more pro-immigrant on this item (59%) than all Western European nations except Britain (62%) but slightly less than Canadians and Australians. The US also falls in the middle of the pack on a question from the same survey about whether the country should encourage highly skilled people to immigrate and work there (78%) – an idea supported by large majorities of all publics in Europe and the settler nations.[6] The US falls modestly but noticeably lower than many of its peers on the question of whether to take in refugees from countries where people are fleeing violence and war. Although 66% of Americans supported this, the figure is lower than in Australia (73%), Britain (74%), and Canada (74%) and quite a bit lower than in Germany (82%) and France (79%).

Still, on the same survey, several items display either uniquely high American optimism about immigration or put the US in a class exclusive or near exclusive to the other settler nations. The US ranks highest (54%) among all developed nations Pew surveyed on agreement that "immigrants in our country today want to adopt" the country's "way of life." Even Australians and Canadians are less certain, at 44% and 48% respectively. And while some of Europe achieves similar scores (France and Sweden are at 51% each), most score notably lower (Spain at 46%, Britain at 43%, Germany at 33%, and Italy at a mere 10%).

Asked whether their country should let in more immigrants than now, about the same, or fewer, the US (24%) was second only to Spain (28%) in the number saying immigration levels should be increased and tied with Canada for lowest number saying the level should be decreased (25%). The US public was significantly more pro-immigrant on this question than Australia (18 increase to 37 decrease) as well as all EU countries sampled other than Spain,

American Exceptionalism?

with which it tied – Britain (16–35), France (16–40), Germany (10–54), Italy (5–56), Netherlands (10–38), Sweden (14–51).

Finally, despite the distinctive salience of illegal immigration in US politics during the Trump era, the US ranked dead last in support for deporting those in the country without permission (46%) – substantially lower than Canada (53%), Australia (61%), and Britain (57%) and far lower than two countries that register quite pro-immigrant on other measures, Germany (73%) and Sweden (73%). This parallels the *relatively* lax attitude in the US toward border control that we observed in the ISSP. Americans surely want border security, but despite the sustained rhetoric about migrant caravans, states of emergency, and walls, they are less supportive of draconian measures to stem the tide than are citizens in countries with lower levels of illegal immigration and much less political heat around the issue. It is noteworthy, too, that the US stands out, sometimes alone, often in combination with the other settler nations or at least Canada, even on surveys that do not include any questions that tap into what the ISSP battery shows to be the most distinctively American orientations toward immigration – a thin and pluralistic conception of assimilation, identity, and membership, paired with an insistence that these choices be left to individuals rather than controlled by government.

Summary

We rate the claim that America is an exceptional nation when it comes to mass opinion about immigration "Mostly True." To summarize, there is substantial evidence that Americans follow their own path in forming opinions about immigration and immigrants, differing not only from Europe but also from other countries sharing similar immigrant backgrounds. At the same time, the other settler nations have been and remain as or more supportive of immigration in certain respects, though these comparisons are complicated by the fact that these nations confront less illegal entry and use points systems to base selection

Immigration in the Court of Public Opinion

of immigrants heavily on skill. Americans are among the most accepting of large-scale immigration flows, least strident about strong enforcement measures on illegal immigration, more sanguine about the *consequences* of immigration, and they are exceptional above all in their laissez-faire outlook on the role of cultural diversity in their society.

6

Conclusion

Public opinion about immigration has taken on greater political significance during an era in which debates over admissions, enforcement, and immigrant rights have become more partisan and polarized.[1] Once carried on by lobbyists, technocrats, and their congressional allies behind the closed doors of K Street conference rooms and Capitol Complex offices,[2] immigration policy-making has sprung into public view, with images of marches, border crossings, and human smuggling widely available on television and social media.[3] How, then, do Americans, who readily call themselves a nation of immigrants, think and feel about immigration?

To move beyond the impressionistic mantras routinely served up by activists, pundits, and politicians, we have let the public speak for itself through numerous public opinion polls. These surveys, spanning the period before, during, and after the Trump presidency, query citizens' beliefs about who and how many should be admitted, the economic and social consequences of immigration, feelings about illegal entry and the agencies charged with administering immigration law, preferences over a wide range of immigration policy alternatives, and conceptions of what immigrants owe their new nation and what the nation owes them in return. The results of our review of the polls brought into relief the public's conceptions of how immigration is reshaping the political community and what these herald for beliefs about what it means to be an American.

119

Immigration in the Court of Public Opinion

In this concluding chapter, we first review the key findings from our exploration and then turn to the bedeviling question of what role public opinion about immigration plays in shaping elite debates and channeling the course of policy. In so doing, we re-examine the conventional wisdom that the US immigration system is dysfunctional or "broken."[4] Public support is only one yardstick by which to measure a policy's success, but in a democracy, it is an important one. Despite Americans' obvious dissatisfaction with the status quo, our findings suggest that many of the reform proposals being pushed by the right, left, and center would do little to quell discontent and might well increase it. Unambiguously popular reforms are for the moment hostage to uncompromising brinkmanship by activists whose agendas are deeply out of sync with mass opinion. With ordinary citizens now a pivotal audience in immigration debates, advocates of reform need to consider not only which changes to tout but also how to frame them. Building robust support for the elusive goal of comprehensive immigration reform will require that leaders move beyond the question of *whether* it is politically expedient to talk about immigration to a sober appraisal of *how* to talk about it.

The Evidence of the Polls

The conventional storyline in accounts of America's immigration history portrays a cycle of backlash, accommodation, and acceptance. Immigration introduces "strangers" into "our" land whose cultural and racial differences from the native majority portend irreversible changes to the nation's security, prosperity, and way of life. Nativist reactions follow, unleashing fear and loathing toward the newcomers and a spate of efforts to restrict immigration and limit the rights of immigrants. Against the odds, the immigrants prove their mettle and stake out their slice of the American dream. Anxieties subside. The engine of assimilation gradually erodes differences to the point that the outsiders become insiders. The cultural mainstream is enriched and invigorated by the immigrants' cultural and economic contributions. Finally,

Conclusion

"they" become part of "us," even *joining* in the hostile reaction to the next wave of those pushed by poverty and oppression to seek a better life in the land of opportunity. Films such as *The Emigrants, Fiddler on the Roof, Brooklyn, America, America,* and *The Namesake* capture the pain and promise of coming to America of diverse groups from different eras.

This schematic periodization has its shortcomings and glosses over the nuance and diversity of public opinion and policy responses that exists in every age. But suppose that we accept it as a rough approximation of the truth. Where in the cycle are we now? The overwhelming view among the pundits is that the backlash phase is in full swing. Personified by Donald Trump and earlier anti-immigrant political wannabes such as Patrick J. Buchanan, this reactionary movement reaches its fever pitch in racist theories of the "Great Replacement" of whites by non-whites from the developing world who are eagerly ushered in and then manipulated by coastal elites to forsake traditional American values, stub out the country's white majority, and undermine the ability of "natives" to earn a decent living by the sweat of their brow.[5] The supposed backlash against immigration is evidenced by chants of "Build the Wall," demeaning rhetoric about "illegals" and "criminal aliens," and even "merit-based immigration," which political figures as prominent as House Speaker Nancy Pelosi have decried as "condescending" and part of a plan to "make America white again."[6] Those who see a backlash in full swing also tend to regard a coalition of well-heeled cosmopolitans and racial minorities as the only bulwark against nativist designs to turn back the clock to the 1920s, when racist national origins quotas stemmed the tide of what 1880 Census director and then MIT president Francis Walker called "beaten men from beaten races; representing the worst failures in the struggle of existence."

One can easily draw a line all the way from Benjamin Franklin's description of Germans as "palatine boors" in the early days of the Republic, to Samuel Morse's anti-Popery in the 1830s and '40s, to Henry Cabot Lodge's Social Darwinist broadsides against Southern and Eastern European immigration in the 1920s, to George Kennan's lament as late as 2002 that Latin American

Immigration in the Court of Public Opinion

immigration amounted to the nation's identity being "recklessly trashed in favor of a polyglot mix-mash,"[7] to candidate Trump's never-retracted bluster about Mexican rapists and drug dealers.

But survey evidence lends no support whatsoever to the notion that these nativist sentiments have attracted a large following among contemporary Americans. Nor is it the case that support for open-borders or hard multiculturalist ideology has penetrated beyond a sliver of the US public.

On the contrary, we saw in chapters 1 and 2 that support for immigration has risen dramatically on multiple dimensions since the mid-1990s – a period that much more closely fits the "backlash" label than the current era. And in chapters 2 and 3, we showed that the more rigid and uniform pro- and anti-immigration platforms of some partisan leaders and the most vocal activists are badly out of step with the attitudes of most Americans. Almost all ordinary citizens support some policies that would expand immigration and immigrant rights along with others that would restrict them. Almost all see a mix of positive, neutral, and negative consequences from immigration as it relates to the economy, the culture, and crime.

Relative to Trump's agenda, the public's lean is decidedly pro-immigrant, offering strong support for a path to citizenship, evincing little appetite for major cuts to immigration flows, preferring overwhelmingly to increase skilled immigration but with lukewarm support at best for offsetting cuts to family-based admissions. The dominant body of opinion firmly opposes any semblance of the hardline cruelty of measures such as the separation of apprehended children from their parents – a position from which even Trump eventually retreated while seeking to pin it on the Obama administration. Accordingly, although Trump's positions on immigration helped carve a niche that won him pluralities in pivotal winner-take-all contests during the 2016 primaries, they very likely *cost* him significant support in the general election.[8]

But relative to the positions staked out by pro-immigration activists and an unprecedented number of 2020 Democratic presidential hopefuls, the public's lean is decidedly more restrictive,

Conclusion

eschewing the decriminalization of illegal entry and rejecting the notion that there is no meaningful difference between legal and illegal immigration. There is little consistent backing for large-scale increases in immigration flows, and support for a path to citizenship for illegal immigrants generally is contingent on assimilation criteria and enforcement benchmarks. Moreover, the moderate overall tone and the complexity of opinion is similar across the racial, class, partisan, age, and geographic categories commonly invoked as repositories of either staunch support for or firm opposition to immigration. This nuanced pattern of opinion applies to whites and non-whites, college graduates and non-college voters, Democrats and Republicans, young and old, and rural and urban dwellers. There are, of course, divisions along demographic and political lines. But in comparing these salient social groups across a range of immigration issues, we find that opinions are not nearly as polarized as journalists and politicians often make them out to be. And these opinions are not set in stone. Individuals frequently change their minds about how many immigrants to admit and with what rights and expectations. Aggregate opinion shifts a great deal over time and in response to arguments and information that clarify which values immigration policy alternatives elicit.

Opinions about immigration are tied to both cultural and economic considerations, though on the latter the evidence is stronger for the influence of perceptions about the impact of immigrants on the national economy rather than on narrower pocketbook concerns of individual voters. Ethnic stereotypes clearly play a sizable role in underpinning immigration attitudes. Yet experimental evidence suggests that what matters most to most people is their understanding of how policies conform to the core values of twenty-first-century American political culture – equality, the rule of law, individualism, and humanitarian concerns. When push comes to shove, the cultural concern that predominates in people's minds is the perceived congruence of policies with these values. Prejudicial stereotypes continue to influence choices where policy-related information is scarce. Prejudice seemingly aimed primarily at Hispanics remains an important force in the politics

123

Immigration in the Court of Public Opinion

of immigration, but we find little evidence that most people's thinking about immigration is based on an overriding sense of solidarity with one's own racial in-group or an ideology of white supremacy.

Americans' main expectations of immigrants are that they should assimilate by learning English, working hard to support themselves, and adopting the core national values of freedom and equality of opportunity. They accept that mainstream culture evolves as new ingredients are added to the melting pot and that immigrants may retain pride in their original traditions. But they see the maintenance of those customs as a largely voluntary matter, without an appropriate role for government in either coercing acculturation or promoting multiculturalism. Although many elites in the academy and journalism have embraced a hard multiculturalist ideology portraying assimilation as oppression akin to cultural erasure,[9] most Americans from all ethnic groups endorse the thin version of becoming an American described above. Native-born Americans largely do not demand that immigrants become well versed in American history and civics, celebrate American holidays, or conform in dress and cuisine as conditions of acceptance. And though immigrants are expected to be patriotic and feel American, even smaller minorities of the public apply the British politician Norman Tebbit's "cricket test" that immigrants must root for the national sports team rather than that of their home country as proof that they belong. Though there are partisan and ideological differences, the main story is that belief in the compatibility of patriotism and affection for one's country of origin is broadly shared across political lines, racial groups, and by immigrants themselves. Far from polarization, these beliefs about assimilation represent a remarkable consensus.

There are perennial worries, of course, that *this* wave of immigrants will not follow earlier ones in finding a home in American society because of their insurmountable distinctiveness, the prevalence of one linguistic group, the persistence of enclaves, changes in the structure of the labor market, or the ascendancy of multiculturalism in the academy and other elite institutions that deplore assimilation.[10] These concerns continue to be aired about

Conclusion

Hispanic immigrants and are perhaps at their most acute with respect to Muslims, who continue to face more open and stubborn suspicion than other groups, as the conjoint experiment described in chapter 3 showed.

The reality, however, is that today's immigrants are assimilating in much the same way as their European predecessors. Comparing immigrant generations as we did in chapter 4 makes this clear. The third generation much more closely resembles the native-born whites usually taken as the mainstream standard than earlier generations. Even as many immigrants continue to celebrate their ethnic heritages, over time they overwhelmingly do learn English, participate in the labor force at higher rates than US natives, almost uniformly endorse core liberal values, and display a high degree of patriotism. Hyphenated identities became normal in the melting-pot era of the middle of the twentieth century, and they remain so. But, when the chips are down, among the great majority of recent immigrants it is the American side of the hyphen that proudly outweighs the ethnic in political matters where the two come into tension.

As the demographer Dowell Myers has observed, Americans' worries about the assimilation of current immigrants and their offspring in part reflect a "Peter Pan syndrome" wherein people observe the persistence of large numbers of immigrants who do not yet speak English and have limited familiarity with the host society and infer that this means integration is not taking place. The mistake is in assuming that "immigrants" or "Hispanic immigrants" or "Asian immigrants" are static groups when in fact their composition is constantly changing. Generational change is crucial.[11] By any definition assimilation occurs over time. As immigrants blend in, marry natives, and acculturate, they become less visibly "different."[12] Were Americans more familiar with the facts of assimilation, they would likely be even more supportive of immigration than they currently are, a possibility supported by some recent experimental evidence. That these facts are not well known reflects not only the demagoguery of right-wing anti-immigrant entrepreneurs but the habit of mass media across the political spectrum to essentialize immigrants' ethnic identity and

Immigration in the Court of Public Opinion

cast it as fixed over time and across generations, ignoring the dynamism characteristic of the American ethnic kaleidoscope.

Public commentary about immigration often focuses on the supposedly exclusionary attitudes of ordinary citizens, conflating unhappiness with the government's failure to cope with illegal immigration with rejection of immigration *per se*. In fact, this nation of immigrants stands out for its sanguine attitudes about immigration and lack of enthusiasm for restriction. The US is one of four Anglo-American settler states whose identity is intrinsically tied to its immigrant heritage. These nations see less threat from immigration to the fabric of society and more of an upside than do European democracies. The publics in the settler nations are more likely to accept higher levels of immigration, and, while worried about illegal immigration, they are less in favor of draconian measures to enforce existing immigration laws.

Where American exceptionalism is most evident is in the sphere of beliefs about assimilation. Here Americans prove to be distinct not only from Europe but also from the other settler nations. The hallmark of assimilation American style is a belief that immigrants can have their cake (be it a babka, panettone, tres leches, or chien chang go) and eat it too. They become functional members of the host society through acculturation and economic progress but can preserve their ancestral customs and identifications without sacrificing full membership in their new land. These liberal attitudes about cultural pluralism are entwined with the belief that it is up to individuals, not the government, to shore up waning cultural practices and sustain group boundaries and identities.

None of this squares with the portrait of a rapidly unfolding xenophobic backlash against immigration and immigrants. Of course, there are highly publicized cases of hate and violence. A recent wave of anti-Asian incidents is a recent reprehensible example. But it is worth remembering that ethnocentrism and ethnic conflict are everywhere, perhaps in some sense an innate human tendency. What is clear is that most Americans have nonetheless accommodated and accepted contemporary immigration. Doubtless, if given a choice, they might want to tweak the system, but apparently not by much. Support for family

Conclusion

reunification as a principal basis for allocating visas is a tacit recognition that the Hispanic and Asian populations will continue to grow.

Trump's victory in 2016 has been described as a response to a crisis of American identity, a tussle between its civic creed and the echoes of a bygone era's ethno-nationalism that still reverberate in many people's hearts and minds.[13] If so, the culture war is between domestic enemies, rather than natives and immigrants. The prevailing conception of America that we find in ordinary citizens' opinions about immigration and assimilation is decidedly civic and becoming ever more so, even if the taint of ethnic stereotypes still survives. Given the broader liberalizing trends in the political culture toward embrace of cultural diversity, non-conformity, and lifestyle choice, it is unlikely that this broad accommodation and acceptance of immigration will give way. With apologies to the late, great Yogi Berra, this is not "déjà vu all over again." Superficial rhetorical similarities notwithstanding, the 2020s are not a recurrence of the 1920s. And though Berra sagely cautions us that "It's tough to make predictions, especially about the future," the smart money – barring the proverbial act of God – would bet against a return to nativism and racial quotas.

Of course, immigration will continue nonetheless to roil American politics during the Biden presidency and beyond. Global crises pose the question of how many refugees to admit, and policies may vary according to the cause and source of the push for admissions – read Ukraine versus Haiti. A more permanent issue is the huge increase in attempts to cross the Southern border and the explosion of apprehensions there in 2021. It is unclear how much Biden's promise to reverse Trump's harsh treatment of the would-be migrants contributed to what is widely viewed as a "crisis" with electoral implications, but border control remains as salient an issue as ever. So far, to the dismay of many activists, steps to undo Trump's policies have been measured, and the Biden administration has even defended some of its predecessors' asylum initiatives in court – a testament to the delicate balancing act involved in liberalizing policy while avoiding the political

127

Immigration in the Court of Public Opinion

blowback in store for a president who appears to be letting things spiral out of control.[14]

Coda: Public Opinion, Politics, and Policy

A thorough exploration of the complex relationship between mass opinion and immigration policy is beyond the scope of this book. Nonetheless, the characteristics of contemporary opinion about immigration suggest some important clues about why efforts to achieve comprehensive immigration reform have repeatedly faltered despite the widespread perception that the immigration system is "broken." The Simpson-Mazzoli Act of 1986 was an attempt to reach a compromise over illegal immigration. Legalization of some along with employer sanctions to stem the tide of illegal immigration failed. In 1990, George H.W. Bush proposed reducing the number of legal admissions, a position favored by the public; Congress did the opposite. In 2007, George W. Bush came close to achieving comprehensive reform, but again was stymied, largely because of resistance to proposals regarding illegal immigration. Here we might note the finding that there is a large bloc of "categorical" opponents of anything that smacks of amnesty. Their intense opposition to change has been rewarded by the normal modus operandi of the American system.

Politics is not about the enactment of ideals so much as the weighing of imperfect alternatives. Discontent with the outputs of the political system is not only endemic in American society but inherent in the design of the polity. Pointing to the disharmony generated by the tensions among a moralistic nation's high ideals, its status quo-oriented institutions, and the crooked timber of human nature, Samuel Huntington summed up the enduring American dilemma as follows: "Being human, Americans have never been able to live up to their ideals; being Americans, they have also been unable to abandon them."[15] Elite polarization has accentuated this disharmony in the domain of immigration policy. Americans do not much like the status quo, but their elected

Conclusion

representatives seem incapable of presenting alternatives they would like better.

When it comes to immigration reform, the ship of state is caught between the Scylla of activist demands and the Charybdis of public opinion. The situation is best understood through the lens of what V.O. Key Jr. called "opinion dikes."[16] Clusters of strong opinion check and channel the direction of policy even if they do not usually direct it. These dikes are built from the opinions of elites, organized pressure groups, and ordinary citizens alike. As an example, what Key termed a "permissive" majority prevails regarding two pillars of all recent comprehensive immigration reform proposals that administrations from both parties have pressed since the last large-scale amnesty in 1986: a pathway to citizenship for immigrants in the country without permission and an increase in highly skilled immigration. Both proposals enjoy supermajority support in the public. But when we delve into the details, neither is easily squared with the demands of polarized activists.

On the political left, politicians have bowed to the demands of activists to avoid restricting eligibility for legalization programs to subsets of immigrants such as "Dreamers" and those who have demonstrated self-sufficiency, a modicum of integration, and absence of a criminal record. To many Americans, the defense of sanctuary cities and opposition to a hard line on illegal immigration emanates a faint odor of open borders. On the right, elected officials fear running afoul of the sizable minority of their constituents who view large-scale amnesty, especially with few strings attached, as an assault on fairness and the rule of law. After the political fiasco of the Gang of Eight's effort at immigration reform in 2013 – a shot in the dark that helped deny both Marco Rubio and immigration hardliner Ted Cruz the GOP presidential nomination three years later – Republican leaders have preferred to play it safe and appease the most anti-immigrant elements in their electoral base.

A natural compromise would satisfy the public's egalitarian and humanitarian interest in bringing millions of second-class citizens out of the shadows and preventing a rapid resurgence of

Immigration in the Court of Public Opinion

illegal immigration. But the compromise package of stricter border control and employer sanctions – the core of the 1986 Simpson-Mazzoli grand bargain that passed legislative muster but wound up unfolding as an amnesty with little enforcement – has been off the table. Fearing the loss of bargaining power, the hard left rejects any move toward increasing admission based on high-end skills that is not accompanied by increases in family-based and refugee admissions as well as a comprehensive path to citizenship for illegal immigrants. And the hard right demands that an increase in highly skilled migration levels be combined with sharp reductions in family-based immigration, a divisive position that runs up against Americans' sympathy for the principle of family unity. In short, entrenched interests reject major components of reform that, standing alone, enjoy widespread public support. In its turn, the public rejects the packages offered by their leaders, who are shackled by the preferences of their most intense policy demanders.

These challenges are compounded by a political system laden with "veto points." The treacherous road to reform wends through congressional committees and subcommittees, a super-majoritarian threshold in a malapportioned Senate, the presidential veto, judicial review, and federalism – a thorny issue in immigration policy-making during the nineteenth century that has reasserted itself in the wake of frustration over federal inaction. As a result, an unpopular status quo limps on, while changes that enjoy significant public support fall by the wayside, readily avoided by risk-averse elected officials rather than grappled with head-on.

To proclaim that activists must retool their preferred policy programs and reorient their appeals is to shout into the void. But those advocating liberalizing reforms to admissions and an orderly and humane protocol for dealing with illegal immigration now have at their backs the tailwind of a decades-long shift from the backlash of the 1990s to the accommodation and acceptance of immigration that prevails in our time. Their ability to persuade the public will depend on whether they can resist the temptation to push so far that they run into the headwinds of strong public opposition to policies of multiculturalism and quasi-open

Conclusion

borders that call into question the nation's core values, unity and sovereignty.

To break through the opinion dikes that hold back the preferences of a permissive majority from coming to legislative fruition will require mobilizing mass opinion in a way that elected officials no longer find it in their interest to do, preferring to pander solely to the demands of extreme constituencies. This means transforming a permissive majority for certain immigration reform proposals into a directive one that forces leaders' hands, something that typically happens when a tsunami-like event galvanizes public attention and coalesces opinion in favor of immediate corrective action.

Absent such a shock, change will require a new approach to engaging and persuading an understandably wary, but nevertheless receptive, public. The Trump era spawned a fresh round of debates among public intellectuals about whether politicians – and Democrats in particular – should talk about immigration and other racial issues in making their pitch to voters.[17] Self-styled "popularists" such as David Shor and Matthew Yglesias argue that they do so at their peril, and that they are better off focusing on bread-and-butter issues that elide or downplay controversies related to race and ethnicity. Their critics sensibly counter that the reality is that one side can choose whether to talk or remain silent but not what the conversation is about. Where the advocates of liberalizing reforms to immigration policy choose to talk about other things, their opponents are sure to fill the vacuum, and their claims will go unchallenged. What's more, it is unreasonable in the present era to suppose that politicians can proceed quietly on an issue as potentially explosive as immigration and hope against hope that the public will fail to take notice. In a competitive system, one's opponents will make sure they do.

The question is not whether leaders should talk about immigration but how they can do so in a way that amplifies and energizes public support for specific proposals. Immigration is not a monolith but a panoply of policies and impressions. Public opinion is a mixture of views, positive about some policies, negative about others. Proceeding incrementally by advancing measures with majority, usually bipartisan, public support is

Immigration in the Court of Public Opinion

likelier to succeed than negotiating another grand bargain. The Dream Act and increases to immigration based on needed skills are broadly popular, so pragmatic political leaders should show courage and push for them, pointing to their majority support.

To convince the public that they should care about immigration reform, one can appeal to the values and norms that a broad majority of the public and voters of all demographic and political stripes espouse. This means recognizing that most Americans see illegal immigration as a serious problem, even if many or most illegal immigrants who have lived in the country for years are hardworking, law-abiding people who deserve to be accepted into the national community. Acknowledging this would be a step toward drowning out the chants of "no human is illegal" and screeds about criminal invasions. It means accepting that the public will support mass immigration but only if they are confident that the rules for legalization, admission, and naturalization are consistent with prevailing national values and that they will be enforced.

Politicians should take seriously the public's continued belief in the facts of immigrants' work ethic, English-speaking, and attachment to America and American values, and the remarkable growth of multiracial families. They should trumpet the reality of assimilation. The old story of immigrant absorption has been repeating itself, and misinformation about this can and should be refuted. The fear that immigration is threatening national unity and cultural cohesion is a canard. The real threat comes from within: the elevation by a coterie of activists, academics, and corporate leaders of group identities over a common identity, the racialization of everything, and the creeping erosion of respect for democratic norms and civil discourse.

In the court of public opinion, acceptance of immigration has grown markedly. Absent a major external shock, the current regime of an expansive legal admissions system operating mostly on auto-pilot and benign neglect regarding illegal immigration can limp along largely unaltered, tossing off the slings and arrows hurled from all sides. But to move forward and implement long-stymied immigration reforms that the public favors, leaders must

Conclusion

highlight how policy change can reinforce core American values, and craft narratives that show how today's immigrants want to live the American Creed rather than to undermine it. They need not only to remind Americans that they are a nation of immigrants but also to convince them that immigrants have the will and drive to further the ideal of *e pluribus unum*. The evidence in this book is that Americans will be receptive to this message. They need to hear it and to know that most of their fellow citizens are sympathetic too.

Notes

I Who Are We Now?

1 Maria Sacchetti. "ICE, CPS to Stop Using 'Illegal Alien' and 'Assimilation' under New Biden Administration Order." *Washington Post*, April 19, 2021.

2 Center for Migration Studies. "President Biden's Executive Actions on Immigration." At https://cmsny.org/biden-immigration-executive-actions.

3 Sullivan, Eileen, and Oscar Lopez. "Mexico to Allow US 'Remain in Mexico' Asylum Policy to Resume." *New York Times*, December 2, 2021, https://www.nytimes.com/2021/12/02/us/politics/asylum-seekers-immigration-mexico-usa.html.

4 Dauvergne, Catherine. *The New Politics of Immigration in Settler Societies*. New York: Cambridge University Press, 2016.

5 Key, V.O. Jr. *Public Opinion and American Democracy*. New York: Alfred A. Knopf, 1961.

6 Wood, Gordon S. *The Radicalism of the American Revolution*. New York: Vintage Books, 1993, p. ix.

7 Higham, John. *Strangers in the Land: Patterns of American Nativism, 1860–1925*. New Brunswick, NJ: Rutgers University Press, 2011.

8 Fuchs, Lawrence H. *The American Kaleidoscope: Race, Ethnicity, and the Civic Culture*. Middletown, CT: Wesleyan University Press, 1990.

9 Higham, *Strangers in the Land*, pp. 131–57.

10 Pickus, Noah. *True Faith and Allegiance: Immigration and American Civic Nationalism*. Princeton, NJ: Princeton University Press, 2009, p. 90.

11 Alba, Richard. *The Great Demographic Illusion: Majority, Minority, and the Expanding American Mainstream*. Princeton, NJ: Princeton University Press, 2020, chapter 6.

12 Waldinger Roger, and Mehdi Bozorgmehr (eds.) *Ethnic Los Angeles*. New York: Russell Sage Foundation, 1996.

13 Budiman, Abby. "Key Findings about U.S. Immigrants." Pew Research Center,

Notes to pages 9–16

September 22, 2020, https://www.pewresearch.org/fact-tank/2020/08/20/key-findings-about-u-s-immigrants.

14 Cited in ibid.

15 Ibid.

16 Alba, *The Great Demographic Illusion.*

17 Budiman, "Key Findings about U.S. Immigrants."

18 Hollinger, David A. *Postethnic America: Beyond Multiculturalism.* New York: Basic Books, 2006.

19 Schuck, Peter H. "The Disconnect between Public Attitudes and Policy Outcomes on Immigration." In Carol M. Swain (ed.) *Debating Immigration.* New York: Cambridge University Press, 2007, pp. 17–31.

20 Ibid.

21 Schuck, Peter H. *Citizens, Strangers, and In-Betweens: Essays on Immigration and Citizenship.* New York: Routledge, 2018.

22 Ibid., chapter 1.

23 Krogstad, Jens Manuel. "Americans Broadly Support Legal Status for Immigrants Brought to the U.S. Illegally as Children." Pew Research Center, June 17, 2020, https://www.pewresearch.org/fact-tank/2020/06/17/americans-broadly-support-legal-status-for-immigrants-brought-to-the-u-s-illegally-as-children.

24 Singer, Audrey. "Who Are the DAPA-Eligible Population?" Brookings, December 29, 2014, https://www.brookings.edu/blog/the-avenue/2014/12/29/who-are-the-dapa-eligible-population.

25 See https://www.nilc.org/issues/daca/litigation-related-to-daca. Note that we have focused here on national policy. States and localities have been an important locus of immigration policy-making throughout American history and remain so today, both on the pro- and anti-immigrant side of the ledger. See Schuck, Peter H. "Taking Immigration Federalism Seriously." *University of Chicago Legal Forum* 4, 2007: 57–92.

2 Moderation, Malleability, and the Myth of Warring Camps

1 For examples of such accounts, see Jonathan Haidt's pieces, "When and Why Nationalism Beats Globalism." *The American Interest*, August 8, 2017, https://www.the-american-interest.com/2016/07/10/when-and-why-nationalism-beats-globalism, and "The Ethics of Globalism, Nationalism, and Patriotism." Center for Humans & Nature, September 22, 2016, https://www.humansandnature.org/the-ethics-of-globalism-nationalism-and-patriotism, as well as Michael Lind's "The Open-Borders 'Liberaltarianism' of the New Urban Elite." *National Review*, September 15, 2016, https://www.nationalreview.com/2016/09/open-borders-ideology-american-urban-elite-threaten-nationalism.

2 Gest, Justin. *The New Minority: White Working Class Politics in an Age*

Notes to pages 18–36

of Immigration and Inequality. New York: Oxford University Press, 2018. Hochschild, Arlie R. *Strangers in Their Own Land: Anger and Mourning on the American Right.* New York: Basic Books, 2006.

3 Suro, Roberto, and Marcelo Suárez-Orozco. "From Ellis Island to an Electrified Fence, Why America is So Torn on Immigration." *Washington Post,* October 21, 2011.

4 See, Levy, Morris, Matthew Wright, and Jack Citrin. "Mass Opinion and Immigration Policy in the United States: Re-Assessing Clientelist and Elitist Perspectives." *Perspectives on Politics* 14(3), 2016: 660–80. The Pew Research Center has asked a similar question that does include the word "legal." Support for immigration on that question tends to be modestly higher than on items that do not explicitly differentiate. The trends over time on the standard level of immigration item used in the ANES (and the long-running Gallup series) are quite similar to Pew, however.

5 The wording was "Cities that arrest illegal immigrants for crimes should be required to turn them over to immigration authorities."

6 In the 2019 Cato survey, 53% opposed allowing "immigrants" to receive government financial assistance and services. But this question elides illegal immigrants, legal permanent residents, and immigrants who have become US citizens. Levy and Wright show that there is overwhelming support for naturalized citizens' eligibility for welfare benefits, bare majority opposition to legal permanent residents' eligibility, and overwhelming opposition to furnishing any benefits other than emergency medical care to illegal immigrants. See Levy, Morris, and Matthew Wright. *Immigration and the American Ethos.* New York: Cambridge University Press, 2020. Citrin et al. also report approximately 80% support during the 1990s for requiring legal immigrants to wait at least five years before becoming eligible for welfare benefits – which is in line with current federal policy. See Citrin, Jack, Donald P. Green, Christopher Muste, and Cara Wong. "Public Opinion toward Immigration Reform: The Role of Economic Motivations." *Journal of Politics* 59(3), 1997: 858–81.

7 Citrin et al., "Public Opinion toward Immigration Reform"; Hopkins, Daniel. "Politicized Places: Explaining Where and When Immigrants Provoke Local Opposition." *American Political Science Review* 104(1), 2010: 40–60.

8 For commentary that views bipartisanship in 2013 as limited, see Jeong, Gyung-Ho. "Congressional Politics of U.S. Immigration Reforms: Legislative Outcomes under Multidimensional Negotiations." *Political Research Quarterly* 66(3), 2013: 600–14; and Jeong, Gyung-Ho, Gary J. Miller, Camilla Schofield, and Itai Sened. "Cracks in the Opposition: Immigration as a Wedge Issue for the Reagan Coalition." *American Journal of Political Science* 55(3), 2011: 511–25.

9 See http://www.cnn.com/TRANSCRIPTS/1705/28/sotu.01.html.

10 Hopkins, Daniel, John Sides, and Jack Citrin. "The Muted Consequences

Notes to pages 36–44

of Correct Information about Immigration." *Journal of Politics* 81(1), 2019: 315–20. Kustov, Alexander, Dillon Laaker, and Cassidy Reller. "The Stability of Immigration Attitudes: Evidence and Implications." *Journal of Politics* 83(4), 2021: 1478–94.

11 Levy and Wright, *Immigration and the American Ethos.*
12 Hopkins et al., "The Muted Consequences."
13 Druckman, James N., Erik Peterson, and Rune Slothuus. "How Elite Polarization Affects Public Opinion Formation." *American Political Science Review* 107(1), 2013: 57–79.
14 Grigorieff, Alexis, Christopher Roth, and Diego Ubfal. "Does Information Change Attitudes toward Immigrants?" *Demography* 57, 2020: 1117–143.
15 Williamson, Scott, Claire L. Adida, Adeline Lo, Melina R. Platas, Lauren Prather, and Seth H. Werfel. "Family Matters: How Immigrant Histories Can Promote Inclusion." *American Political Science Review* 115(2), 2021: 686–93.
16 Kalla, Joshua, and David Broockman. "Reducing Exclusionary Attitudes through Interpersonal Conversation: Evidence from Three Field Experiments." *American Political Science Review* 114(2), 2020: 410–25.
17 We do not reproduce the time series here, but it is available at https://news.gallup.com/poll/1660/immigration.aspx.
18 See, for example, Freeman, Gary P., "Modes of Immigration Politics in Liberal Democratic States." *International Migration Review* 29(4), 1994: 881–902.

3 Motivations

1 Malhotra, Neil, Yotam Margalit, Y., and Cecilia Mo. "Economic Explanations for Opposition to Immigration: Distinguishing Prevalence and Conditional Impact." *American Journal of Political Science* (57), 2013: 391–410.
2 Citrin et al., "Public Opinion toward Immigration Reform."
3 Dancygier, Rafaela, and Michael Donnelly. "Sectoral Economies, Economic Contexts, and Attitudes toward Immigration." *Journal of Politics* 75, 2013:17–35; Hainmueller, Jens, and Daniel Hopkins. "The Hidden American Immigration Consensus: A Conjoint Analysis of Attitudes toward Immigrants," *American Journal of Political Science* 59, 2014: 529–48.
4 Citrin et al., "Public Opinion toward Immigration Reform"; Hopkins, "Politicized Places."
5 Levy, Morris, and Matthew Wright. "Economic Self-Interest in Public Opinion about Immigration." Forthcoming.
6 Hainmueller, Jens, and Daniel Hopkins. "Public Attitudes toward Immigration," *Annual Review of Political Science* 17, 2014: 225–49.
7 Ibid.; Ceobanu, Alin, and Xavier Escandell. "Comparative Analyses of Public Attitudes toward Immigrants and Immigration Using Multinational

Notes to pages 45–68

Survey Data: A Review of Theories and Research." *Annual Review of Sociology* 36, 2010: 309–28.

8 Abrajano, Maria, and Zoltan Hajnal. *White Backlash: Immigration, Race, and American Politics.* Princeton, NJ: Princeton University Press, 2015; Gest, *The New Minority*; Jardina, Ashley. *White Identity Politics.* New York: Cambridge University Press, 2019; Kaufmann, Eric. *White Shift.* London: Harry N. Abrams, 2019.

9 Valentino, Nicholas, Ted Brader, and Ashley Jardina. "Immigration Opposition among U.S. Whites: General Ethnocentrism or Media Priming of Attitudes about Latinos?" *Political Psychology* 34, 2013: 149–66; Sides, John, and Kimberley Gross. "Stereotypes, Muslims, and Support for the War on Terror." *Journal of Politics* 75(3), 2013: 583–98; Kalkan, Kerem Ozan, Geoffrey Layman, and Eric Uslaner, 2009. "'Bands of Others'? Attitudes toward Muslims in Contemporary American Society." *Journal of Politics* 71(3), 2009: 847–62.

10 Rubin, Jennifer. "Opinion: The Claims of Anti-Immigrant Hysterics Are Disproved – Again." *Washington Post*, September 28, 2017, https://www.washingtonpost.com/blogs/right-turn/wp/2017/09/28/the-claims-of-anti-immigrant-hysterics-are-disproved-again.

11 Levy and Wright, *Immigration and the American Ethos*.

12 In most conjoint analysis, the respondent is forced to choose one or the other. As we discuss below, we added the flexibility to choose neither or both so that we could identify the kinds of respondents who take a "categorical" view of admitting legal immigrants or giving legal status to illegal immigrants – choosing to accept all ten or reject all ten profiles that they saw.

13 We focus here on poll questions that ask about relative priority or trade-offs without indicating a cut or increase in the total level of legal immigration.

14 In this chapter, we focus only on the issue of legal immigration, but it is possible that the way Americans trade off skills against family varies when the topic turns to illegal immigration. An April 2007 Gallup poll asked whether priority should be given to "highly educated and skilled workers or people who have family members living in the United States" when deciding which illegal immigrants should be given legal status. Here, family (49%) received *more* support than skills and education (38%). The common framing of deportation as "tearing families apart" may have led respondents to prioritize family unity more strongly in this domain than when considering legal admissions.

15 See https://www.bloomberg.com/news/articles/2013-02-21/obama-rated-at-3-year-high-in-poll-republicans-at-bottom. Previewing the results described below in the main text, almost as many (24%) said family reunification should be prioritized as favored high-skilled immigration, while 18% were uncertain.

Notes to pages 71–77

4 Assimilation Then and Now

1 Glazer, Nathan, and Daniel Moynihan. *Beyond the Melting Pot: The Negroes, Puerto Ricans, Jews, Italians, and Irish of New York City.* Cambridge, MA: MIT Press, 1971.

2 Jacoby, Tamar. "Rainbow's End: A Renowned Student of America's Maladies Detects a New Threat to Our Identities." *Washington Post,* May 16, 2004; Alba, Richard D., and Victor Nee. *Remaking the American Mainstream: Assimilation and Contemporary Immigration.* Cambridge, MA: Harvard University Press, 2005.

3 Huntington, Samuel P. *Who Are We? The Challenges to America's National Identity.* New York: Simon & Schuster, 2004. See the discussion in Citrin, Jack, Amy Lerman, Michael Murakami, and Kathryn Pearson. "Testing Huntington: Is Hispanic Immigration a Threat to American Identity?" *Perspectives on Politics* 5(1), 2007: 31–48.

4 Alba and Nee, *Remaking the American Mainstream*; Portes, Alejandro, and Rumbaut, Rubén G. *Legacies: The Story of the Immigrant Second Generation.* Berkeley: University of California Press, 2001.

5 Gordon, Milton M. *Assimilation in American Life: The Role of Race, Religion and National Origins.* New York: Oxford University Press, 2010.

6 Salins, Peter D. *Assimilation, American Style.* New York: Basic Books, 1997.

7 Alba, *The Great Demographic Illusion.*

8 Gans, Herbert J. "Symbolic Ethnicity: The Future of Ethnic Groups and Cultures in America." *Ethnic and Racial Studies* 2(1), 1979: 1–20; Waters, Mary C. *Ethnic Options: Choosing Identities in America.* Berkeley: University of California Press, 2009.

9 Portes, Alejandro, and Min Zhou. "The New Second Generation: Segmented Assimilation and Its Variants." *The ANNALS of the American Academy of Political and Social Science* 530(1), 1993: 74–96; Portes and Rumbaut, *Legacies: The Story of the Immigrant Second Generation.*

10 Telles, Edward, and Christina A. Sue. *Durable Ethnicity: Mexican Americans and the Ethnic Core.* New York: Oxford University Press, 2019; Duncan, Brian, and Trejo, Stephen, "Who Remains Mexican? Selective Ethnic Attrition and the Intergenerational Progress of Mexican Americans," chapter 7 in Lear, David L. and Stephen J. Trejo (eds.) *Latinos and the Economy.* New York: Springer, 2010. See also Alba, *The Great Demographic Illusion.*

11 Alba and Nee, *Remaking the American Mainstream.*

12 Roosevelt, Theodore. *Theodore Roosevelt Papers: Series 2: Letters Sent, –1919; Subseries 3A: Carbon Copies of Letters Sent, 1894 to 1919; Vol. 198, 1919, Jan. 1–Feb. 5.* 1919. Manuscript/Mixed Material, https://www.loc.gov/item/mss382990680.

13 Glazer and Moynihan, *Beyond the Melting Pot.*

14 Lee, Joon. "Arizona Diamondbacks Unveil Gold City Connect Jersey, Referencing Sonoran Desert, Hispanic Culture." ESPN Internet Ventures,

139

Notes to pages 79–90

June 13, 2021, https://www.espn.com/mlb/story/_/id/31623658/arisona-diamondbacks-unveil-gold-city-connect-jersey-referencing-sonoran-desert-hispanic-culture.

15 Lopez, Mark Hugo, Ana Gonzalez-Barrera, and Gustavo López. "Hispanic Identity Fades across Generations and Immigrant Connections Fall Away." Pew Research Center, December 20, 2017, https://pewresearch.org/hispanic/2017/12/20. The figures below are taken from this excellent study.

16 Ibid.

17 We are indebted to Emily Ekins for providing access to these data and permission to report them. The Cato report is authored by Emily Ekins and David Kemp: "E Pluribus Unum: Findings from the Cato Institute 2021 Immigration an Identity Survey."

18 Cited in Citrin, Jack, and David O. Sears. *American Identity and the Politics of Multiculturalism*. New York: Cambridge University Press, 2014, p. 10.

19 Lien, Pei-te, M. Margaret Conway, and Janelle Wong. *The Politics of Asian Americans: Diversity and Community*. New York: Routledge, 2004.

20 For technical reasons we could not perform this calculation for the Cato survey.

21 Citrin and Sears used a different measure of identity choice, asking: "When it comes to politics and social affairs, do you think of yourself mainly as a member of your racial or ethnic group, as just an American, or both?" In a series of Los Angeles County surveys reported in *American Identity and the Politics of Multiculturalism* they find a very similar pattern of results across ethnic groups and immigrant generations.

22 Suro, Roberto. *Strangers Among Us: How Latino Immigration is Transforming America*. New York: Alfred A. Knopf, 1999.

23 Duncan, Brian, and Stephen J. Trejo. "Intermarriage and the Intergenerational Transmission of Ethnic Identity and Human Capital for Mexican Americans." *Journal of Labor Economics* 29(2), 2011: 195–227.

24 Lopez, Mark Hugo, Ana Gonzalez-Barrera, and Gustavo López. "Latino Identity Declines across Generations as Immigrant Ties Weaken." Pew Research Center's Hispanic Trends Project, September 22, 2020.

25 Citrin, Jack, Beth Reingold, and Donald P. Green. "American Identity and the Politics of Ethnic Change." *Journal of Politics* 52(4), 1990: 1124–54; Schildkraut, Deborah J. *Americanism in the Twenty-First Century: Public Opinion in the Age of Immigration*. New York: Cambridge University Press, 2011; Theiss-Morse, Elizabeth. *Who Counts as American? The Boundaries of National Identity*. New York: Cambridge University Press, 2009.

26 Citrin and Sears, *American Identity and the Politics of Multiculturalism*, pp. 171–2.

27 Silver, Laura, Moira Fagan, Aidan Connaughton, and Mara Mordecai. "Views about National Identity Becoming More Inclusive in U.S., Western Europe," Pew Research Center, May 5, 2021, https://www.pewresearch.org

Notes to pages 92–119

/global/2021/05/05/views-about-national-identity-becoming-more-inclusive -in-us-western-europe. The International Social Survey Program (ISSP) of the National Opinion Research Center (NORC) of the University of Chicago has asked these "true national identity" questions in cross-national surveys conducted in 1995, 2003, and 2013.

28 Citrin and Sears, *American Identity and the Politics of Multiculturalism*, pp. 191–2.

29 McRee, Nick, and Mark Setzler. "The Civic Orientation and Political Assimilation of Latino Immigrant Youth." *Sociological Focus* 52(3), 2019: 246–66.

30 A full discussion of the Multicultural Policy Index and related issues can be found at https://www.queensu.ca/mcp/about.

31 Citrin, Jack, David O. Sears, Christopher Muste, and Cara Wong. "Multiculturalism in American Public Opinion." *British Journal of Political Science* 31(2), 2001: 247–75.

32 Citrin and Sears, *American Identity and the Politics of Multiculturalism*, chapter 5.

33 Sacchetti, "ICE, CBP to Stop Using 'Illegal Alien' and 'Assimilation' under New Biden Administration Order."

34 Goldberg, Zach. "America's White Saviors." *Tablet*, June 5, 2019, https:// www.tabletmag.com/sections/news/articles/americas-white-saviors.

5 American Exceptionalism?

1 Quoted in Kazin, Michael. "The Right's Unsung Prophet," *The Nation* 248, February 20, 1989, p. 242.

2 Hainmueller and Hopkins, "Public Attitudes toward Immigration."

3 Ceobanu and Escandell. "Comparative Analyses of Public Attitudes toward Immigrants."

4 For a good overview of "American Exceptionalism" in historiographical and social-scientific terms, see Shafer, Byron E. "American Exceptionalism." *Annual Review of Political Science* 2(1), 1999: 445–63.

5 See https://news.gallup.com/poll/320678/world-grows-less-accepting -migrants.aspx.

6 See https://www.pewresearch.org/global/question-search/?qid=2942&cnt IDs=&stdIDs=.

6 Conclusion

1 Wong, Tom K. *The Politics of Immigration: Partisanship, Demographic Change, and American National Identity*. New York: Oxford University Press, 2017.

2 Tichenor, Daniel J. *Dividing Lines: The Politics of Immigration Control in*

Notes to pages 119–128

America. Princeton, NJ: Princeton University Press, 2002. Freeman, "Modes of Immigration Politics in Liberal Democratic States."

3 Tichenor, Daniel J. "Navigating an American Minefield: The Politics of Illegal Immigration." *The Forum* 7(3), 2009; Levy and Wright, *Immigration and the American Ethos*.

4 See, for example, Bahar, Dany. "The Road to Fix America's Broken Immigration System Begins Abroad." Brookings, December 8, 2020, https://www.brookings.edu/blog/up-front/2020/12/08/the-road-to-fix-americas-broken-immigration-system-begins-abroad; Bier, David. "Why the Legal Immigration System Is Broken: A Short List of Problems." Cato Institute, July 10, 2018, https://www.cato.org/blog/why-legal-immigration-system-broken-short-list-problems; Ries, Lora. "Securing the Border and Fixing Our Broken Immigration System." The Heritage Foundation, September 21, 2020, https://www.heritage.org/immigration/commentary/securing-the-border-and-fixing-our-broken-immigration-system.

5 Charlton, Lauretta. "What Is the Great Replacement?" *New York Times*, August 6, 2019, https://www.nytimes.com/2019/08/06/us/politics/grand-replacement-explainer.html. Skolnik, Jon. "How the 'Great Replacement' Theory Went from Charlottesville to the GOP Mainstream." Salon, September 29, 2021, https://www.salon.com/2021/09/29/what-is-the-great-replacement-theory-and-why-is-it-gaining-ground-within-the-gop.

6 Schwartz, Ian. "Pelosi: Trump Immigration Plan a Campaign to 'Make America White Again.'" Real Clear Politics, January 27, 2018, https://www.realclearpolitics.com/video/2018/01/27/pelosi_trump_immigration_plan_a_campaign_to_make_america_white_again.html#.

7 Kauffman, Bill. *Bye Bye, Miss American Empire: Neighborhood Patriots, Backcountry Rebels, and Their Underdog Crusades to Redraw America's Political Map*. White River Junction, VT: Chelsea Green Pub. Co., 2010.

8 Mutz, Diana C. "Status Threat, Not Economic Hardship, Explains the 2016 Presidential Vote." *Proceedings of the National Academy of Sciences* 115(19), 2018: E4330–9.

9 Glenn, Evelyn Nakano. "Settler Colonialism as Structure." *Sociology of Race and Ethnicity* 1(1), 2015: 52–72.

10 Huntington, Samuel P. "The Hispanic Challenge." *Foreign Policy*, October 28, 2009, https://foreignpolicy.com/2009/10/28/the-hispanic-challenge.

11 Myers, Dowell. *Immigrants and Boomers*. New York: Russell Sage Foundation, 2007.

12 Alba, *The Great Demographic Illusion*.

13 Packer, George. *Last Best Hope: America in Crisis and Renewal*. New York: Farrar, Straus and Giroux, 2021. Sides, John, Michael Tesler, and Lynn Vavreck. *Identity Crisis: The 2016 Presidential Campaign and the Battle for the Meaning of America*. Princeton, NJ: Princeton University Press, 2019.

14 Kanno-Youngs, Zolan. "Biden Administration Fights in Court to Uphold

Notes to pages 128–131

Some Trump-Era Immigration Policies." *New York Times*, March 13, 2022, https://www.nytimes.com/2022/03/13/us/politics/biden-trump-immigration. html.

15 Huntington, Samuel P. "American Ideals versus American Institutions." *Political Science Quarterly* 97(1), 1982: 1.

16 Key, *Public Opinion and American Democracy.*

17 Klein, Ezra. "David Shor Is Telling Democrats What They Don't Want to Hear." *New York Times*, October 8, 2021, https://www.nytimes.com/2021 /10/08/opinion/democrats-david-shor-education-polarization.html; Cooper, Ryan. "The Democrats' New Cult of the Popular." Yahoo!, August 5, 2021, https://www.yahoo.com/now/democrats-cult-popular-095808221.html.

References

Abrajano, Marisa, and Zoltan Hajnal. *White Backlash: Immigration, Race, and American Politics*. Princeton, NJ: Princeton University Press, 2015.

Alba, Richard. *The Great Demographic Illusion: Majority, Minority, and the Expanding American Mainstream*. Princeton, NJ: Princeton University Press, 2020.

Alba, Richard D., and Victor Nee. *Remaking the American Mainstream: Assimilation and Contemporary Immigration*. Cambridge, MA: Harvard University Press, 2005.

Bahar, Dany. "The Road to Fix America's Broken Immigration System Begins Abroad." Brookings, December 8, 2020, https://www.brookings.edu/blog/up-front/2020/12/08/the-road-to-fix-americas-broken-immigration-system-begins-abroad.

Bier, David. "Why the Legal Immigration System Is Broken: A Short List of Problems." Cato Institute, July 10, 2018, https://www.cato.org/blog/why-legal-immigration-system-broken-short-list-problems.

Budiman, Abby. "Key Findings about U.S. Immigrants." Pew Research Center, September 22, 2020, https://www.pewresearch.org/fact-tank/2020/08/20/key-findings-about-u-s-immigrants.

Center for Migration Studies, "President Biden's Executive Actions on Immigration," https://cmsny.org/biden-immigration-executive-actions.

Ceobanu, Alin M., and Xavier Escandell. "Comparative Analyses of Public Attitudes toward Immigrants and Immigration Using Multinational Survey Data: A Review of Theories and Research." *Annual Review of Sociology* 36(1), 2010: 309–28, https://doi.org/10.1146/annurev.soc.012809.102651.

Charlton, Lauretta. "What Is the Great Replacement?" *New York Times*, August 6, 2019, https://www.nytimes.com/2019/08/06/us/politics/grand-replacement-explainer.html.

Citrin, Jack, Amy Lerman, Michael Murakami, and Kathryn Pearson. "Testing Huntington: Is Hispanic Immigration a Threat to American

References

Identity?" *Perspectives on Politics* 5(1), 2007, https://doi.org/10.1017/s1537592707070041.

Citrin, Jack, Beth Reingold, and Donald P. Green. "American Identity and the Politics of Ethnic Change." *Journal of Politics* 52(4), 1990: 1124–54, https://doi.org/10.2307/2131685.

Citrin, Jack, and David O. Sears. *American Identity and the Politics of Multiculturalism*. New York: Cambridge University Press, 2014.

Citrin, Jack, David O. Sears, Christopher Muste, and Cara Wong. "Multiculturalism in American Public Opinion." *British Journal of Political Science* 31(2), 2001: 247–75, https://doi.org/10.1017/s0007123401000102.

Citrin, Jack, Donald P. Green, Christopher Muste, and Cara Wong. "Public Opinion toward Immigration Reform: The Role of Economic Motivations." *Journal of Politics* 59(3), 1997: 858–81, https://doi.org/10.2307/2998640.

Cooper, Ryan. "The Democrats' New Cult of the Popular." Yahoo!, August 5, 2021, https://www.yahoo.com/now/democrats-cult-popular-095808221.html.

Dancygier, Rafaela M., and Michael J. Donnelly. "Sectoral Economies, Economic Contexts, and Attitudes toward Immigration." *Journal of Politics* 75(1), 2013: 17–35, https://doi.org/10.1017/s0022381612000849.

Dauvergne, Catherine. *The New Politics of Immigration and the End of Settler Societies*. New York: Cambridge University Press, 2016.

Dorning, Mike. "Obama Rated at 3-Year High in Poll Republicans at Bottom." Bloomberg, February 21, 2013, https://www.bloomberg.com/news/articles/2013-02-21/obama-rated-at-3-year-high-in-poll-republicans-at-bottom.

Druckman, James N., Erik Peterson, and Rune Slothuus. "How Elite Partisan Polarization Affects Public Opinion Formation." *American Political Science Review* 107(1), 2013: 57–79, https://doi.org/10.1017/s0003055412000500.

Duncan, Brian, and Stephen J. Trejo. "Intermarriage and the Intergenerational Transmission of Ethnic Identity and Human Capital for Mexican Americans." *Journal of Labor Economics* 29(2), 2011: 195–227, https://doi.org/10.1086/658088.

Duncan, Brian, and Stephen J. Trejo. "Who Remains Mexican? Selective Ethnic Attrition and the Intergenerational Progress of Mexican Americans." In David L. Leal and Stephen J. Trejo (eds.) *Latinos and the Economy*. New York: Springer, 2010, 285–320.

Ekins, Emily, and David Kemp, "E Pluribus Unum: Findings from the Cato Institute 2021 Immigration an Identity Survey." Cato Institute, Washington D.C., 2021.

Esipova, Neli, Julie Ray, and Anita Pugliese. "World Grows Less Accepting of Migrants." Gallup, November 20, 2021, https://news.gallup.com/poll/320678/world-grows-less-accepting-migrants.aspx.

Freeman, Gary P. "Modes of Immigration Politics in Liberal Democratic States." *International Migration Review* 29(4), 1994: 881–902, https://doi.org/10.2307/2547729.

References

Fuchs, Lawrence H. *The American Kaleidoscope: Race, Ethnicity, and the Civic Culture*. Hanover, CT: Wesleyan University Press, 1995.

Gans, Herbert J. "Symbolic Ethnicity: The Future of Ethnic Groups and Cultures in America." *Ethnic and Racial Studies* 2(1), 1979: 1–20.

Glazer, Nathan, and Daniel P. Moynihan. *Beyond the Melting Pot: The Negroes, Puerto Ricans, Jews, Italians, and Irish of New York City*. Cambridge, MA: MIT Press, 1971.

Glenn, Evelyn Nakano. "Settler Colonialism as Structure." *Sociology of Race and Ethnicity* 1(1), 2015: 52–72, https://doi.org/10.1177/2332649214560440.

Goldberg, Zach. "America's White Saviors." *Tablet*, June 5, 2019, https://www.tabletmag.com/sections/news/articles/americas-white-saviors.

Gordon, Milton M. *Assimilation in American Life: The Role of Race, Religion and National Origins*. New York: Oxford University Press, 2010.

Grigorieff, Alexis, Christopher Roth, and Diego Ubfal. "Does Information Change Attitudes toward Immigrants?" *Demography* 57(3), 2020: 1117–43, https://doi.org/10.1007/s13524-020-00882-8.

Haidt, Jonathan. "The Ethics of Globalism, Nationalism, and Patriotism." Center for Humans & Nature, September 22, 2016, https://www.humansandnature.org/the-ethics-of-globalism-nationalism-and-patriotism.

Haidt, Jonathan. "When and Why Nationalism Beats Globalism." *The American Interest*, August 8, 2017, https://www.the-american-interest.com/2016/07/10/when-and-why-nationalism-beats-globalism.

Hainmueller, Jens, and Daniel J. Hopkins. "The Hidden American Immigration Consensus: A Conjoint Analysis of Attitudes toward Immigrants." *American Journal of Political Science* 59(3) (2015): 529–48, https://doi.org/10.2139/ssrn.2106116.

Hainmueller, Jens, and Daniel J. Hopkins. "Public Attitudes toward Immigration." *Annual Review of Political Science* 17 (2014): 225–49, https://doi.org/10.2139/ssrn.2289270.

Higham, John. *Strangers in the Land: Patterns of American Nativism, 1860–1925*. New Brunswick, NJ: Rutgers University Press, 2011.

Hochschild, Arlie Russell. *Strangers in Their Own Land: Anger and Mourning on the American Right*. New York: The New Press, 2016.

Hollinger, David A. *Postethnic America: Beyond Multiculturalism*. New York: Basic Books, 2006.

Hopkins, Daniel J. "Politicized Places: Explaining Where and When Immigrants Provoke Local Opposition." *American Political Science Review* 104(1), 2010: 40–60, https://doi.org/10.1017/s0003055409990360.

Hopkins, Daniel J., John Sides, and Jack Citrin. "The Muted Consequences of Correct Information about Immigration." *Journal of Politics* 81(1), 2019: 315–20, https://doi.org/10.2139/ssrn.2798622.

Huntington, Samuel P. "American Ideals versus American Institutions." *Political Science Quarterly* 97(1), 1982: 1, https://doi.org/10.2307/2149312.

References

Huntington, Samuel P. "The Hispanic Challenge." *Foreign Policy*, October 28, 2009, https://foreignpolicy.com/2009/10/28/the-hispanic-challenge.

Huntington, Samuel P. *Who Are We? The Challenges to America's National Identity*. New York: Simon & Schuster, 2005.

Jacoby, Tamar. "Rainbow's End: A Renowned Student of America's Maladies Detects a New Threat to Our Identities." *Washington Post*, May 16, 2004.

Jardina, Ashley. *White Identity Politics*. New York: Cambridge University Press, 2019.

Jeong, Gyung-Ho. 2013. "Congressional Politics of U.S. Immigration Reforms: Legislative Outcomes under Multidimensional Negotiations." *Political Research Quarterly* 66(3): 600–14.

Jeong, Gyung-Ho, Gary J. Miller, Camilla Schofield, and Itai Sened. "Cracks in the Opposition: Immigration as a Wedge Issue for the Reagan Coalition." *American Journal of Political Science* 55(3), 2011: 511–25.

Kalkan, Kerem Ozan, Geoffrey C. Layman, and Eric M. Uslaner. "'Bands of Others'? Attitudes toward Muslims in Contemporary American Society." *Journal of Politics* 71(3), 2009: 847–62, https://doi.org/10.1017/s0022381609090756.

Kalla, Joshua L., and David E. Broockman. "Reducing Exclusionary Attitudes through Interpersonal Conversation: Evidence from Three Field Experiments." *American Political Science Review* 114(2), 2020: 410–25, https://doi.org/10.1017/s0003055419000923.

Kauffman, Bill. *Bye Bye, Miss American Empire: Neighborhood Patriots, Backcountry Rebels, and Their Underdog Crusades to Redraw America's Political Map*. White River Junction, VT: Chelsea Green Pub. Co., 2010.

Kaufman, Eric. *White Shift: Populism, Immigration, and the Future of White Majorities*. New York, Harry N. Abrams, 2019.

Kazin, Michael. "The Right's Unsung Prophet." *The Nation* 248, February 20, 1989.

Key, Vladimir Orlando Jr. *Public Opinion and American Democracy*. New York: Alfred A. Knopf, 1961.

Klein, Ezra. "David Shor Is Telling Democrats What They Don't Want to Hear." *New York Times*, October 8, 2021, https://www.nytimes.com/2021/10/08/opinion/democrats-david-shor-education-polarization.html.

Krogstad, Jens Manuel. "Americans Broadly Support Legal Status for Immigrants Brought to the U.S. Illegally as Children." Pew Research Center, August 16, 2021, https://www.pewresearch.org/fact-tank/2020/06/17/americans-broadly-support-legal-status-for-immigrants-brought-to-the-u-s-illegally-as-children.

Kustov, Alexander, Dillon Laaker, and Cassidy Reller. "The Stability of Immigration Attitudes: Evidence and Implications." *Journal of Politics* 83(4), 2021: 1478–94, https://doi.org/10.2139/ssrn.3322121.

Lear, David L., and Stephen J. Trejo (eds.) *Latinos and the Economy: Integration and Impact in Schools, Labor Markets, and Beyond*. New York: Springer, 2010.

References

Lee, Joon. "Arizona Diamondbacks Unveil Gold City Connect Jersey, Referencing Sonoran Desert, Hispanic Culture." ESPN Internet Ventures, June 13, 2021, https://www.espn.com/mlb/story/_/id/31623658/arisona-diamondbacks-unveil-gold-city-connect-jersey-referencing-sonoran-desert-hispanic-culture.

Levy, Morris, and Matthew Wright. *Immigration and the American Ethos*. New York: Cambridge University Press, 2020.

Levy, Morris, Matthew Wright, and Jack Citrin. "Mass Opinion and Immigration Policy in the United States: Re-Assessing Clientelist and Elitist Perspectives." *Perspectives on Politics* 14(3), 2016: 660–80.

Lien, Pei-te, M. Margaret Conway, and Janelle Wong. *The Politics of Asian Americans: Diversity and Community*. New York: Routledge, 2004.

Lind, Michael. "The Open-Borders 'Liberaltarianism' of the New Urban Elite." *National Review*, September 15, 2016, https://www.nationalreview.com/2016/09/open-borders-ideology-american-urban-elite-threaten-nationalism.

Lopez, Mark Hugo, Ana Gonzalez-Barrera, and Gustavo López. "Latino Identity Fades across Generations as Immigrant Connections Fall Away." Pew Research Center, December 20, 2017, https://www.pewresearch.org/hispanic/2017/12/20/hispanic-identity-fades-across-generations-as-immigrant-connections-fall-away.

McRee, Nick, and Mark Setzler. "The Civic Orientation and Political Assimilation of Latino Immigrant Youth." *Sociological Focus* 52(3), 2019: 246–66, https://doi.org/10.1080/00380237.2019.1624231.

Malhotra, Neil, Yotam Margalit, and Cecilia Hyunjung Mo. "Economic Explanations for Opposition to Immigration: Distinguishing between Prevalence and Conditional Impact." *American Journal of Political Science* 57(2), 2013: 391–410, https://doi.org/10.1111/ajps.12012.

Mutz, Diana C. "Status Threat, Not Economic Hardship, Explains the 2016 Presidential Vote." *Proceedings of the National Academy of Sciences* 115(19), 2018: E4330–9, https://doi.org/10.1073/pnas.1718155115.

Myers, Dowell. *Immigrants and Boomers*. New York: Russell Sage Foundation, 2007.

Packer, George. *Last Best Hope: America in Crisis and Renewal*. New York: Farrar, Straus and Giroux, 2021.

Pickus, Noah. *True Faith and Allegiance: Immigration and American Civic Nationalism*. Princeton, NJ: Princeton University Press, 2009.

Portes, Alejandro, and Min Zhou. "The New Second Generation: Segmented Assimilation and Its Variants." *The ANNALS of the American Academy of Political and Social Science* 530(1), 1993: 74–96.

Portes, Alejandro, and Rumbaut, Rubén G. *Legacies: The Story of the Immigrant Second Generation*. Berkeley: University of California Press, 2001.

"Question Search." Pew Research Center's Global Attitudes Project. Pew Research Center, June 24, 2019, https://www.pewresearch.org/global/question-search/?qid=2942&cntIDs=&stdIDs=.

References

Ries, Lora. "Securing the Border and Fixing Our Broken Immigration System." The Heritage Foundation, September 21, 2020, https://www.heritage.org/immigration/commentary/securing-the-border-and-fixing-our-broken-immigration-system.

Roosevelt, Theodore. *Theodore Roosevelt Papers: Series 2: Letters Sent, –1919; Subseries 3A: Carbon Copies of Letters Sent, 1894 to 1919; Vol. 198, 1919, Jan. 1–Feb. 5.* 1919. Manuscript/Mixed Material, https://www.loc.gov/item /mss382990680.

Rubin, Jennifer. "Opinion: The Claims of Anti-Immigrant Hysterics Are Disproved – Again." *Washington Post*, September 28, 2017, https://www.washingtonpost.com/blogs/right-turn/wp/2017/09/28/the-claims-of-anti-immigrant-hysterics-are-disproved-again.

Sacchetti, Maria. "ICE, CBP to Stop Using 'Illegal Alien' and 'Assimilation' under New Biden Administration Order." *Washington Post*, April 19, 2021, https://www.washingtonpost.com/immigration/illegal-alien-assimilation/2021 /04/19/9a2f878e-9ebc-11eb-b7a8-014b14aeb9e4_story.html.

Salins, Peter D. *Assimilation, American Style.* New York: Basic Books, 1997.

Schildkraut, Deborah J. *Americanism in the Twenty-First Century: Public Opinion in the Age of Immigration.* New York: Cambridge University Press, 2011.

Schuck, Peter H. *Citizens, Strangers, and In-Betweens: Essays on Immigration and Citizenship.* New York: Routledge, 2018.

Schuck, Peter H. "The Disconnect between Public Attitudes and Policy Outcomes on Immigration." In Carol M. Swain (ed.) *Debating Immigration.* New York: Cambridge University Press, 2007, pp. 17–31.

Schuck, Peter H. "Taking Immigration Federalism Seriously." *University of Chicago Legal Forum* 4, 2007: 57–92.

Schwartz, Ian. "Pelosi: Trump Immigration Plan a Campaign to 'Make America White Again.'" Real Clear Politics, January 27, 2018, https://www.realclearpolitics.com/video/2018/01/27/pelosi_trump_immigration_plan _a_campaign_to_make_america_white_again.html#!

Shafer, Byron E. "American Exceptionalism." *Annual Review of Political Science* 2(1), 1999: 445–63, https://doi.org/10.1146/annurev.polisci.2.1.445.

Sides, John, and Kimberly Gross. "Stereotypes, Muslims, and Support for the War on Terror." *Journal of Politics* 75(3), 2013: 583–98, https://doi.org/10 .1017/s0022381613000388.

Sides, John, Michael Tesler, and Lynn Vavreck. *Identity Crisis: The 2016 Presidential Campaign and the Battle for the Meaning of America.* Princeton, NJ: Princeton University Press, 2019.

Silver, Laura, Moira Fagan, Aidan Connaughton, and Mara Mordecai. "Views about National Identity Becoming More Inclusive in U.S., Western Europe." Pew Research Center, May 5, 2021, https://www.pewresearch.org/global/2021 /05/05/views-about-national-identity-becoming-more-inclusive-in-us-western -europe.

References

Singer, Audrey. "Who Are the Dapa-Eligible Population?" Brookings, December 29, 2014, https://www.brookings.edu/blog/the-avenue/2014/12/29/who-are-the-dapa-eligible-population.

Skolnik, Jon. "How the 'Great Replacement' Theory Went from Charlottesville to the GOP Mainstream." Salon, September 29, 2021, https://www.salon.com/2021/09/29/what-is-the-great-replacement-theory-and-why-is-it-gaining-ground-within-the-gop.

Sullivan, Eileen, and Oscar Lopez. "Mexico to Allow U.S. 'Remain in Mexico' Asylum Policy to Resume." *New York Times*, December 2, 2021.

Suro, Roberto. 1999. *Strangers Among Us: How Latino Immigration is Transforming America*. New York: Alfred A. Knopf.

Suro, Roberto, and Suárez-Orozco, Marcelo. "From Ellis Island to an Electrified Fence, Why America is So Torn on Immigration." *Washington Post*, October 21, 2011.

Telles, Edward, and Christina A. Sue. *Durable Ethnicity: Mexican Americans and the Ethnic Core*. New York: Oxford University Press, 2019.

Theiss-Morse, Elizabeth. *Who Counts as American? The Boundaries of National Identity*. New York: Cambridge University Press, 2009.

Tichenor, Daniel J. *Dividing Lines: The Politics of Immigration Control in America*. Princeton, NJ: Princeton University Press, 2002.

Tichenor, Daniel J. "Navigating an American Minefield: The Politics of Illegal Immigration." *The Forum* 7(3), 2009, https://doi.org/10.2202/1540-8884.1325.

Valentino, Nicholas A., Ted Brader, and Ashley E. Jardina. "Immigration Opposition among U.S. Whites: General Ethnocentrism or Media Priming of Attitudes about Latinos?" *Political Psychology* 34(2), 2013: 149–66, https://doi.org/10.1111/j.1467-9221.2012.00928.x.

Waldinger, Roger, and Mehdi Bozorgmehr (eds.) *Ethnic Los Angeles*. New York: Russell Sage Foundation, 1996.

Waters, Mary C. *Ethnic Options: Choosing Identities in America*. Berkeley: University of California Press, 2009.

Williamson, Scott, Claire L. Adida, Adeline Lo, Melina R. Platas, Lauren Prather, and Seth H. Werfel. "Family Matters: How Immigrant Histories Can Promote Inclusion." *American Political Science Review* 115(2), 2020: 686–93, https://doi.org/10.1017/s0003055420001057.

Wong, Tom K. *The Politics of Immigration: Partisanship, Demographic Change, and American National Identity*. New York: Oxford University Press, 2017.

Wood, Gordon S. *The Radicalism of the American Revolution*. New York: Vintage, 1993.

Index

Page numbers in *italics* refer to a table/figure

affirmative action 93
Africa 103, 115
African Americans
  legal emancipation of 8
  see also blacks
age
  as immigrant attribute 62, 63, *64*,
    65, 65
  public opinion based on 29
aggregate change 38–40
Alba, Richard 74
American Civil War 6
American Creed 5, 11, 133
American exceptionalism 99–118
  and assimilation 114, 126
  consequences of immigration
    106–9, *107*
  and cultural pluralism 109–14,
    110, 113
  definition 99
  evidence 101–3
  and government support for
    maintaining minority culture
    112–14, *113*
  inflows and border controls 103–6,
    104
  into the Trump era 114–17
American identity
  attributes and what makes a "true"
    American 89–92, *91*

and being native born 90, *91*
and ethnic identification 4–5,
  10–1, 79, 80–5, *82, 84, 85, 86,*
  87–9
factors transitioning from foreign
  to 89
generational differences 83, *84, 85,*
  89
and level of immigration 87
and speaking English 85, 90–2, *91,*
  95, 96
American National Election Studies
  see ANES
"Americanization" of immigrants 73,
  75, 88
ANES (American National Election
  Studies) surveys 69
  (2012) 40
  (2016) 78–9, 80–9
  (2020) 18–29, 35, 45–57, 78–9,
    80–9, 92
  weaknesses of 47, 56–7
Anglo-Conformity 4
anti-Asian incidents 126
anti-immigrant parties
  rise of in Europe 112
anti-immigration sentiment 4, 12, 15,
  38–9, 39, 52
  grounding of in racism 45–6
Arizona Diamondbacks 77

151

Index

Asian immigrants 29–30, 52, 97–8
  and American/ethnic identity 81,
    83, 85, 86, 87, 88, 89
  anti-Asian incidents 126
  intermarriage with whites 83
  number of 9, 10
  views on assimilation 94–5
  views on what makes a "true"
    American 90, 91
assimilation 3–4, 8, 11, 45, 46, 61–2,
  71–98, 120, 124, 125, 132
  and "Americanization" of
    immigrants 73
  and American exceptionalism 114,
    126
  and American/ethnic identity 79,
    80–8, 82, 84, 86
  cross-country analysis 109–12, 110
  cultural 63, 73, 85, 87, 93
  ethnic affinities retaining their hold
    77
  Huntington on 72
  ideological perspectives 75–9
  importance of immigrants
    displaying certain traits/behaviors
    95–6, 96
  and intermarriage 4, 73, 74, 79,
    83, 89
  liberal 75–6, 80, 95
  meaning 72–4
  monistic view 75–6
  and multiculturalism 76–8, 93–7
  nativist view of 75
  pluralistic 75, 76
  and Roosevelt 7
  segmented 74, 92–3, 98
  straight-line model 73, 74, 79–80
  structural 73, 74
  survey evidence and data 79–81
  thin 77, 95, 114, 117, 124
  views on progress of 94–6, 96
  which version is supported by
    Americans 89–93
attributes, immigrant see immigrant
  attributes
Australia 102, 115, 116, 117
  immigration policy 102
  points system 44

Banting, Keith 93
baseball 77
Berra, Yogi 127
Biden, President 2, 97, 127
bilingualism 80, 91, 92, 93–4
birthright citizenship 19, 22, 24, 25
black civil rights groups 17
blacks 52
  and American/ethnic identity 81, 85
  share of US population 9
  views on assimilation 94–5
  views on immigration 30
  views on what makes a "true"
    American 90, 91
Bloomberg poll (2013) 68
Boehner, John 14
border control/security 21, 25, 103–6,
  104, 117, 127
  decriminalizing illegal crossings 20,
    24
Bracero System 10
Britain 116, 117
Buchanan, Patrick J. 39, 121
Bush, George H.W. 128
Bush, George W. 14, 128

Canada 115, 116, 117
  immigrants' share of population
    102
  immigration policy 102
  migrants from 10
  points system 44
Caribbean 115
Cato Institute's Immigration and
  Identity Survey (2021) 21, 78,
    79, 80, 81, 82, 83, 89, 92, 94,
    95, 98
Census Bureau 9
chain migration 9
child migrants 19, 22
  and birthright citizenship issue 22
  and DACA 2, 14, 22
Chiles, Lawton 39
Chinese Exclusion Act (1882) 6
Chinese immigrants 6, 10, 65
Christian immigrants 65, 66
citizenship
  birthright 19, 22, 24, 25

152

Index

path to for illegal immigrants *19*, 20, 21, 24–5, 35–6, 122, 129, 130
Citrin, Jack 93
Citrin, Jack and Sears, David *American Identity and the Politics of Multiculturalism* 88
Civil Rights Act (1964) 8
civil rights movement 71
class 17, 27–8, 31, 101
Clinton, Bill 39
CNN poll 67–8
Cold War 8
comprehensive immigration reform (CIR) 13–14
conjoint analysis 62
Cooperative Congressional Election Survey (2015) 68
cosmopolitan liberalism 8
country of origin
  identification with 79, 124
  as immigrant attribute 62, *64*, 65, *65*, 69
Crevecoeur
  Letters From an American Farmer 99–100
crime
  and immigration 107–8, *107*
  impact of illegal immigration on 22
Cruz, Ted 129
cultural assimilation 63, 73, 85, 87, 93
cultural motivations 41, 44–7
  group-centric perspective 41, 44–6, 51–4, *53*, 58, 65, 70
  values-centric view 41, 46–7, 54–5, *56*, 58, 70
cultural pluralism 4, 109–14, *113*, 126
  resistance to 3, *110*
"cultural threat" 44–5

DACA program (Deferred Action for Childhood Arrivals) program 2, 14–15, 22, 33
de Tocqueville, Alexis
  Democracy in America 101
Declaration of Independence 99

Deferred Action for Childhood Arrivals *see* DACA program
Deferred Action for Parents of Americans and Lawful Permanent Residents (DAPA) 14
Democrats 17, 20, 25, 32–6, *34*, 51, 98
deportation 13, 21–2, 24, 35, 117
directive consensus 4
diversity visa lottery 20
"double consciousness" 81
Dreamers 40, 63, 99, 129
Dubois, W.E.B. 81
Duncan, Brian 88

Eastern Europe
  immigrants from 7, 8
economic motivations 41, 42–4, 48–51, *50*, *53*, 58
economy
  cross-national opinion of immigration's impact on 107, *107*
education
  bilingual 92, 93–4
  as immigrant attribute 62, 63, *64*, 65, 67–8
  and immigrant selection 42, 44, 103
  public opinion based on 27–9, *28*
egalitarian values 54–5, *56*
El Salvador
  number of immigrants from 10
Emanuel, Rahm 33
employment-based immigration 20
  see also skills-based immigration
English proficiency
  and American/ethnic identity 85, 90–2, *91*, 95, *96*
  as immigrant attribute 61, 62, *64*, 66
ethnic diversity 102, 109
  threatening of national unity concern 71
Ethnic Heritage months 77
ethnic identification 80–90
  relationship with American identity 4–5, 10–11, 79, 80–5, *82*, *84*, 86, 87–9

153

Index

ethno-nationalism 127
ethnocentrism 45, 51, 52, 54, 126
eugenics 7
Europe
  opposition to immigration 43
  see also Western Europe
European Union 115

family-based admissions 44, 70, 83,
  122, 130
family reunification-based
  immigration 8–9, 20, 67–8, 109,
  126–7
federalism 130
"feeling thermometers" 51
"festival" multiculturalism 77–8
Founders 6
France 116, 117
Franklin, Benjamin 121

Gallup polls 11, *12*, 13, 67
  (2013) 67
Gallup World Survey (2016-17)
  Migrant Acceptance Index 115–17
"Gang of Eight" immigration reform
  bill 14, 129
General Social Survey *see* GSS
generational change 125
  and ethnic/American identification
    83, *84*, 85, 89
  and level of immigration 87
  public opinion on immigration 29
geography
  public opinion based on 31–2, *32*
German immigrants 6, 65
Germany 116, 117
Glazer, Nathan 71
  We Are all Multiculturalists Now 78
globalization 17
Goldberg, Zach
  Tablet 98
Gordon, Milton 77
  Assimilation in American Life 73
government support
  for maintaining minority culture
    112–13, *113*
"Great Replacement" theory 121
Green Cards 44, 68

group-centric view 41, 44–6, 51–4,
  53, 58, 59, 65, 70, 85
GSS (General Social Survey) 94
  (2000) 91–2
  (2006-08-10) 36–7
  (2013) 95
  (2020) 37

Hainmueller, Jens 44
Hart-Celler Act (1965) 69
Hartz, Louis 112
Harvard-Harris poll (2017) 20
health insurance 20
hemispheric caps 8, 10
high-skilled immigration 14, 42, 67,
  68
Hispanic immigrants/immigration 3,
  52, 72, 74, 97–8, 125
  and American/ethnic identity 79,
    81, 83, 85, 86, 87, 88, 89
  and English language 92
  and intermarriage 79
  political engagement of young 93
  prejudice against 123–4
  seen as a threat by Huntington 72
  share of US population 9, 10
  views on assimilation 94, 94–5
  views on immigration 30, 30
  views on what makes a "true"
    American 90, 91, 92
Hofstadter, Richard 99
Hopkins, Daniel 38, 44
Huntington, Samuel 92, 128
  Who Are We? 72

Iceland 108, 115
ideas, introduction of new
  and immigration 107, *107*, 108
identity politics 71, 72
illegal immigrants/immigration 4,
  103, 123
  countries compared regarding
    strengthening restrictions on *104*,
    105–6
  DACA program and children of 2,
    14–15, 22, 33
  and deportation 13, 21–2, 24, 35,
    117

154

Index

health insurance and welfare benefits 20, 24
and Immigration Reform and Control Act (1986) 32–3
impact on crime 22
number of 10
opposition to legalization of by the public 66
path to citizenship *19*, 20, 21, 24–5, 35–6, 122, 129, 130
public opinion on 13, *19*, 21–2, 63, 66
and Republicans/Democrats 33
and Simpson-Mazzoli Act (1986) 128, 130
viewed unfavourably 13, 132
Illegal Immigration Reform and Immigrant Responsibility Act 13
immigrant attributes 60–9, *64*, 69–70
age 62, 63, *64*, 65, *65*
country of origin/ethnicity 62, *64*, 65, *65*, 69
education 62, 63, *64*, 65, 67–8
implications for legal immigration policy design 66–7
job performance/skills 14, 42, 62, 63, *64*, 65, 67, 68, 103, 116, 132
language skills/English fluency 61, 62, 63, *64*, 66
religious background 62, *64*, 65, 65–6
Immigration and Customs Enforcement (ICE) 20
Immigration and Nationality Act (1965) 8, 11
immigration policy 128–9
core issues 1
immigration reform 13–15, 129
comprehensive (CIR) 13–14
Gang of Eight's attempt at (2013) 14, 129
and "opinion dikes" 129
and public opinion 13–15
reasons for faltering of 128–31
way forward 131–3
Immigration Reform and Control Act (1986) 32–3

immigration/immigrants
Americans' main expectations of 124
cross-national opinion on consequences of 106–9, *107*
early restriction of in US 102
history of American 5–11
hostility toward and backlash against 1–2, 121
impact of 22
legislation limiting 6, 7–8
mixture of anti and pro attitudes toward 16–17, 22–6, *23*, 26
party polarization over 17
share of US population 9–10, *9*, 102
India
number of immigrants from 10
individualism 47, 99
intermarriage 4, 73, 74, 79, 83, 89
International Social Survey Program *see* ISSP
Ireland 108, 115
Irish immigrants 6
Islam 66
conflation with terrorism 66
ISSP (International Social Survey Program)
National Identity module 101, 102, 103–4, *104*, *107*, 109, *110*, *113*, 114–15, 117
Italy 116, 117

Japanese Americans 80
job skills/performance
and immigrant selection 14, 42, 62, 63, *64*, 65, 67, 68, 103, 116, 132
issuing of Green Card based on 68
jobs
competition with immigrants issue 42–3, 100, 115
cross-national opinion of immigration's impact on 107, *107*
Johnson, Lyndon 8

Kennan, George 121–2
Key Jr, V.O. 4, 129

Index

Know Nothings 6
Kymlicka, Will 93

labor 16
  immigrants and contract 10
  temporary work programs and
    low-skilled 14
  see also jobs
labor unions 17
language rights 91
language skills *see* English proficiency
Latin America 115
Latino/Latin American immigrants/
    immigration 10, 29–30, 65,
    121–2
Lazarus, Emma 7, 74
legislation
  limiting immigration 6, 7–8
level of immigration 24, 116
  economic motivations 48–51, *50*,
    58
  generational differences over views
    of 87
  and group-centric motivations
    51–4, *53*, *58*, *59*
  influence of ethnic identification/
    American identity on views of 87
  malleability of public opinion 36–8
  and motivations 47–60, *50*, *53*, *56*
  public opinion on 11–12, *12*, 21,
    24, 36–7, 39, 58–9, 69
  and Republicans/Democrats 35
  values-based motivations 54–5, *56*,
    58, 60
Levy, Morris and Wright, Matthew
  *Immigration and the American
    Ethos* 59–60
liberal assimilation 75–6, 80, 95
liberalism 70
  cosmopolitan 8
  folk notion of 70
Lodge, Henry Cabot 121
low-skilled workers 68

McRee, Nick 92
majority-minority society 10
Marx, Karl 101
melting pot 7, 73, 76, 89, 94

merit-based immigration 2, 20, 44,
    62, 63, 69, 121
Mexican immigrants 1, 2, 65
  and ethnic identification 74, 88
  number of 10
Mexico
  building a wall on border 21
  contract labor of seasonal migrants
    from 10
Middle East 103
  flood of refugees from 105
Migrant Acceptance Index *see* Gallup
    World Survey
Miller, Stephen 72
minority culture
  government support for 112–13,
    113
Morse, Samuel 121
motivations 41–70
  cultural 41, 44–7, 51–5, *53*, *56*, *58*,
    65, 70
  economic 41, 42–4, 48–51, *50*, *53*
  evidence 47–57
  group-centric 41, 44–6, 51–4, *53*,
    58, *59*, 65, 70, 85
  and immigrant attributes preferred
    60–70, *64*
  improving the evidence through
    survey experiments 57–60
  values-based 41, 46–7, 54–5, *56*,
    58, 70
Moynihan, Daniel 71
multiculturalism/multiculturalists 3, 5,
    11, 72, 76–8, 111, 124
  and assimilation 76–8, 93–7
  cross-country analysis 109–12, *110*
  festival 77–8
  meaning 93
  unpopularity of hard 93–4
Muslim immigrants 65, 66, 111, 125
  antipathy and bias against 1, 2, 3,
    66, 103
Myers, Dowell 125

National Asian American and Pacific
    Islander Survey (2016) 85
national identity *see* American
    identity

156

Index

national origins quota system 7, 61, 121
national welfare reform (1996) 13, 39
native-born Americans 48, 73, 83, 124
native-born, being
  importance to American identity 90, *91*
nativists/nativism 5, 6, 7, 16, 26, 37–8, 39, 40, 70, 75, 77, 80, 96, 98, 100, 120, 121–2
Nee, Victor 74
Netherlands 117
New York Times/CBS poll 67
New Zealand 102, 115
  immigration policy 102
Nigerian immigrants 65
9/11 66, 108

Obama, Barack 14, 22, 33
opinion dikes 129, 131

Pakistani immigrants 65
partisanship
  public opinion based on 32–6, *34*
  and relationship between economic outlook and views on immigration *50*, 51
patriotism 11, 14, 72, 78, 83, 85, 88, 92, 97, 124, 125
PBS New Hour-Marist poll (2019) 20
Pelosi, Nancy 121
permissive consensus 4
persuasion 38
"Peter Pan syndrome" 125
Pew Global Attitudes and Trends (2018) 116
Pew Latino National Survey (2015) 78
Pew Research Center report (2020) 9
Pew Research Center surveys 90
  (2015-16) 79–80, 88
Philippines
  number of immigrants from 10
points system 2, 62, 67, 117–18
  Canadian and Australian 44
policy reform *see* immigration reform

political parties
  polarization over immigration 17
popular culture
  immigration and evolution/ expansion of 77
populists 131
Portes, Alejandro 74
pragmatism 5
"Prosperity Gospel" 99
public opinion
  heterogeneity and moderation in key groups 26–36
  malleability of 36–8
  as moderate and mixed 18–26
  motivations 41–70

race 17
  public opinion based on 29–30, *30*
racism
  and anti-immigration sentiment 45–6
randomization 57–8, *59*
refugees 21
religion 22, 96, 99
  as immigrant attribute 62, *64*, 65–6, *65*
Republicans 17, 32–6, *34*, 39–40, 51, 98, 129
Roosevelt, Theodore 7, 75, 80
Rubin, Jennifer 45
Rubio, Marco 129
rule of law 5, 38, 41, 58, 66, 70, 123, 129
rural–urban divide 31–2, *32*

sanctuary cities 20, 24, 129
Satmar Jews 89
Scandinavia
  on consequences of immigration 107, *107*
  government support for maintaining minority culture *113*
  inflows and border controls *104*, 105
  views on cultural pluralism *110*
Sears, David 88
segmented assimilation 74, 92–3, 98
self-interest, economic 42–3

157

Index

settler states 102–3, 116, 117–18, 126
  and acceptance of migrants 115
  on consequences of immigration 107, *107*
  government support for maintaining minority culture *113*
  inflows and border controls *104*, 105
  multiculturalism versus assimilation 110–11, *110*
  views on consequences of immigration *107*, 108
  views on cultural pluralism 110–11, *110*
  see also Australia; Canada; New Zealand
Setzler, Mark 92
Shor, David 131
Simpson-Mazzoli Act (1986) 128, 130
skills-based immigration 33, 68, 70
  see also job skills/performance
Social Darwinism 7, 121
societal economic thinking 43–4
Southern Europe
  immigrants from 7, 8
Spain 108, 116
stereotypes, ethnic 65, 66, 69, 123, 127
structural assimilation 73, 74
Sue, Christina 74
Suro, Roberto 88
survey experiments 57–60
Survey Sampling International 62
Sweden 115, 116, 117
Switzerland 108

Tebbit, Norman 124
Telles, Edward 74
temporary work programs 14
third-generation immigrants 73, 74, 79, 80, 83, 85, 87, 125
travel ban 15
Trejo, Stephen 88
tribalism 71

"true" American, what makes a 89–92, *91*
Trump, Donald 34, 39, 127, 131
  and American exceptionalism 114–17
  and DACA 14, 22
  immigration policy and views on 1–2, 15, 20, 21, 22, 25, 30, 33, 35, 40, 45, 72, 108, 121, 122
  Make American Great Again slogan 1, 81

underclass 74
United Technologies/National Journal Congressional Connection poll (2013) 67
urban–rural divide 31–2, *32*
utility-maximization 42

values-based motivations 41, 46–7, 54–5, *56*, 58, 70
Voting Rights Act (1965) 8

Walker, Francis 121
warring camps, myth of 16–18
Washington Post/ABC poll (2007) 68
welfare
  and migrants 13, 39, 115–16
Western Europe
  on consequences of immigration 107, *107*
  and cultural pluralism 111–12
  government support for maintaining minority culture *113*
  inflows and border controls 104–5, *104*
  views on cultural pluralism *110*
white working class 33
  views on immigration 27–8, *28*
Wilson, Pete 39
Wood, Gordon 6
World War I 7
World War II 8, 74

Yglesias, Matthew 131

158